SKY SOLDIERS

THE 173RD AIRBORNE BRIGADE IN VIETNAM

CHARLES J. MCARTHUR

CONTENTS

Introduction   V

1. SOUTHEAST ASIA AND THE GROWING THREAT
   OF COMMUNISM   I
   French Colonialism and Japanese Control on the
   Indochina Peninsula   3
   The Events Leading up to the War   7
   Justification for US Involvement in Vietnam   12

2. THE SKY SOLDIERS ENTER VIETNAM   15
   History of the 173rd Airborne Brigade   17
   The Sky Soldiers' Deployment to Vietnam   19
   Arriving in War Zone D   20

3. WAR ZONE D OPERATIONS   23
   Operation HUMP   24
   Operation MARAUDER   28
   Establishing Areas and Dividing the Units   29
   Ending Operation MARAUDER   38
   Operation CRIMP   38

4. OPERATIONS CEDAR FALLS AND JUNCTION
   CITY   41
   Operation CEDAR FALLS   42
   Entering War Zone C   44
   Operation JUNCTION CITY   45
   Planning Operation JUNCTION CITY   45
   The Execution of the Largest Airborne Operation   48
   The End of the Operation   52
   The Parachute and Dagger: The Origins of the
   Unit's Insignia   54
   After Operation JUNCTION CITY   55

5. THE BATTLE OF DAK TO – PART 1   57
   Established Presence in the Region   58
   A Nerve Center for the VC   60
   Operations SAM HOUSTON and FRANCIS
   MARION   62
   Operation GREELEY   65

6. THE BATTLE OF DAK TO – PART 2 HILL 875   69
Operation MACARTHUR   74
Escalation at the Beginning of 1968 – The Tet Offensive   75
Following the Tet Offensive   78
The Steady Fighting through January 1969   79
The Outcome of the Battle of Dak To   80

7. FAMOUS LEADERS OF THE 173RD   83
William R. Peers   84
John R. Deane Jr   86
Leo H. Schweiter   87

8. THE SKY SOLDIERS IN POPULAR CULTURE   91
Citations and Honors   92
173rd Airborne Brigade Memorials   93

Conclusion   95
Vietnam Timeline   99
References   103
About the Author   115

INTRODUCTION

Various fighting formations throughout history have earned a reputation for being efficient and formidable; from the Roman Praetorian Guard to the Janissary of the Ottoman Empire, from the Jaguar Knights of the Aztec Empire to the French Foreign Legion, the names of certain fighting forces echo through the hallowed halls of history and strike fear into the hearts of their enemies while standing for the height of discipline, loyalty, and effectiveness. The 173rd Airborne Brigade, also known as the 'Sky Soldiers', is akin to one of these famous groups.

Before the start of the Vietnam War, the 173rd Airborne had already established a reputation for itself. Even amongst other airborne units, they were known for their effectiveness and zeal. They had a swagger and an attitude that communicated just how confident they were in their abilities. It was not only in how they carried themselves but in the little habits and idiosyncrasies the unit had formed going back to the first world war. By the time 1963 rolled around, and the US was looking for soldiers to send to Vietnam, the 173rd's standing as a bold and ferocious fighting force had already been established.

"To call reveille, the battalion commander of the 2/503rd erected several very large speakers from which the song of the theme to 'Rawhide' was blasted all over their camp. Every morning, the Sky Soldiers of the 173rd's 2/503rd were rousted from their bunks by the blaring words, "Head 'em up, move 'em out, Rawhide" or something to that effect. The entire 173rd Airborne Brigade soon became known as 'the Herd.'"[1]

The Sky Soldiers solidified their legacy during the Vietnam War by participating in various operations, contributing to several successes, and executing the largest airborne operation of the war, all while exhibiting a particular type of intensity and zeal. From Operation JUNCTION CITY to the Battle of Dak To, the Sky Soldiers made a significant impact on the direction of the Vietnam War. This book will explore many of these operations in detail, but it will also include many stories of the individuals who experienced these events.

It might be surprising that the men of the 173rd who fought and died in the jungles of Vietnam were not preoccupied with legacy or legend. The soldiers who were part of this storied group with such a grand tradition were often more focused on one another. What allowed them to be so cavalier was their commitment to one another and the trust they had in their fellow soldiers.

In 1970, for example, Brian Danker did not even know what the 173rd was, but when he saw men from the 173rd, he knew he wanted to be a part of what they were doing. When he ran into a sergeant from the legendary 173rd, he managed to get what he wanted. Danker would find the 173rd to be a transformative experience. In a 2022 interview for the West Point Center for Oral History, he described why the 173rd was so important to him.

"I attribute my survival out of Vietnam because I was with November company [of the 75th Regiment, serving with the 173rd]. The professionalism, the camaraderie, just the knowhow of everyone knowing what their jobs were."[2]

He isn't the only one who relied on his fellow soldiers for safety and success. Another Sky Soldier, Lawrence Boyd, Sr., had similar things to say about serving with the 173rd in Vietnam. While interviewed by D. Kevin McNeir of the Washington Informer in April 2022, he gave his account of a medic attached to the 173rd trying to revive Boyd's mortally wounded friend, Private First Class (PFC) Watson, because of a Viet Cong (VC) ambush during their first patrol assignment:

"He was literally trying to blow life back into Watson and had to eventually be pulled away from him—it was too late. I realized that everyone who was around me during the war was more than just other soldiers—we were family."[3]

This perspective on the 173rd has come up repeatedly over the years. When the Vietnam veterans from the 173rd, all of whom are of retirement age, talk about being Sky Soldiers, the men do not speak of medals or presidential unit citations, though they could. Steve Corey, a ranger with the 75th Infantry Regiment, 175th Airborne, gave an interview in 2022 where he said:

"Any one of us at any given moment could have gotten a medal of honor because if you get into a contact, you may do a heroic thing, but you don't write it down, you don't notify it, it doesn't go forward or anything like that."[4]

Corey explained that what did matter was the people he was

deployed with. He spoke about learning survival techniques from his fellow soldiers, like how to cross his legs properly when he performed parachute jumps or the right way to be the point person on patrol; how the men blew off steam together, sometimes breaking the rules by joyriding in MP jeeps; how the men celebrated together, procuring steaks from back home; and how they mourned their losses together, comforting one another over the passing of a friend. Those moments with fellow soldiers had more to do with being a part of the 173rd than plaudits.

While the 173rd has a legendary reputation and is well-decorated with honors and citations, the soldiers who call themselves members of the Sky Soldiers focus on something else. Men like Brian Danker, Lawrence Boyd, Steve Corey, and many others mentioned in this book have all shared their experiences in the brotherhood of the Sky Soldiers. The stories of these men reveal the camaraderie inherent in being a part of something with tradition, history, and importance.

The men of the 173rd shared a bond. The challenges of Vietnam drew them closer together, and they learned to rely on one another for comfort, success, and survival.

This book is dedicated in particular to the brave soldiers of the 173rd Airborne Brigade, the "Sky Solders," who were the longest-serving soldiers of the Vietnam War and were pivotal to the early successes of the battle for Vietnam. The unit participated in the first major operation of the war, conducted the only operational parachute jump, and fought in some of the fiercest battles until the beginning of 1971.

The Sky Soldiers are a remarkable example of courageous and resilient soldiers, despite facing harrowing experiences and moments of extreme danger. They had the determination that should inspire pride. They fought and died with honor, despite the war's unpopularity back home; their honor can never be questioned or taken from them despite the current ruling classes' preoccupation with re-writing history to meet the morals and values of today.

ix

1

SOUTHEAST ASIA AND THE GROWING THREAT OF COMMUNISM

To better understand the heroic battles of the Sky Soldiers in Vietnam, we must first understand the road to conflict and historical geo-political events that led to the war. This will be addressed over the next chapter to give important context to the Sky Soldiers' involvement.

The events leading up to the Vietnam War and subsequent US involvement began with the waning French influence in the area and the elevation of other powers to fill the resulting vacuum. Various political parties arose, with Ho Chi Minh among the most notable leaders during the 1930s. In September 1940, any internal struggle ceased when Japan invaded the small country as a strategic move to take over China. Vietnam remained under Japanese control until the end of World War II in 1945. Once the threat of foreign invasion was removed, the fight for control of the country resumed, even as the people tried to heal from the oppression of a foreign aggressor.[1]

The end of World War II saw a significant shift in the power structures around the world. Imperialism was in considerable decline and ended in the middle of the century. With the spread of fascism halted, the remaining Allied powers split into the two predominant ideological camps: democracy and communism. These ideologies worked together to end the rise of fascism during the 1940s, but by the 1950s, they viewed each other as antithetical. Most of the western world saw the rise of communism as the next significant threat, with the US being the primary opponent to nations adopting this form of government. However, communism had already become the primary ideology across much of Asia and had been adopted in many regions in the early part of the 20th century before World War II.

Although communism took hold in Asia before World War II, the US decided to prevent communism from taking root again after World War II ended. When the US could not prevent communism from spreading in Korea, President Truman feared communism would spread, similar to how Russia created the USSR—by forcing a communist government on one country after another throughout the region.

The Red Scare was a primary focus of several American presidential administrations. Following his oath of office in November 1963, President Lyndon B. Johnson expressed a fear nearly identical to the one Truman used to justify the US involvement in Korea the previous decade. Johnson told South Vietnam Ambassador Henry Cabot Lodge Jr.,

> "I am not going to lose Vietnam. I am not going to be the president who saw Southeast Asia go the way China went."[2]

This was a controversial statement, as he expressed this sentiment only two days after being sworn in and only two days after President John F. Kennedy was assassinated. Having just lost a president, many Americans weren't ready to consider another military involvement. The fear expressed by the new president also ignored just how much the Vietnamese had done to prevent the rise of a dictatorship in their country. While the

US fretted over what to do, Vietnam fought without any outside assistance.

FRENCH COLONIALISM AND JAPANESE CONTROL ON THE INDOCHINA PENINSULA

Although Great Britain is the nation most closely associated with colonialism, France was nearly an equal imperial power around the same time. During the latter part of the 19th century, France colonized the Indochina Peninsula under the direction of Napoleon III. There had been a call to invade Vietnam, with the French Naval Commander Rigault de Genouilly being one of the most outspoken advocates for the action. His initial orders were to take Tourane (modern-day Da Nang) and convert it into a military base from which the French could push farther inland.

The invading force arrived near the city in August 1858 before launching the invasion on September 1, 1858. It took the French until 1887 to fully control the peninsula, after which they referred to the new French colony as the French Indochinese Union, or French Indochina. France gained complete control of much of the peninsula, including the modern-day nations of Vietnam, Cambodia, and Laos.

These nations had their own history, and each posed a unique challenge to French control. Nevertheless, the region became an essential part of the French colonies, and the French attempted to retain a firm hold over it. They were successful in doing so for roughly six decades, which significantly changed the lives of the people in all the nations on the peninsula. While the French gained considerable economic benefits from controlling the region, they helped to industrialize the region at the same time. Unfortunately, the French were the primary benefactors of the economic gain while the peasants worked the land. Food became increasingly scarce over the early part of the 20th century, and the people who lived there had no say or control over the capitalist system that regulated them. The Vietnamese people had no civil liberties and were struggling economically.

French control was finally lost on September 26, 1940, when Japan invaded the peninsula. To the Japanese Empire, this was a strategic move in the Sino-Japanese War to gain control near the southern border of China, preventing the Chinese from importing arms and fuel through French Indochina along the Kunming-Haiphong railway. While Japanese forces concentrated on the Sino-Japanese War, Japan decided to leave the existing French colonial government in place, and the administration of Vietnam remained the responsibility of the French. World War II raged in the west, and Germany invaded France, leaving the Indochina peninsula vulnerable while France focused on protecting their homeland from the Nazis.

Japanese forces used this opportunity to establish more of a military presence in Vietnam, leaving the French to govern the people. In contrast, Japanese forces prioritized their military presence and furthered their goals against China. The Vietnamese faced being controlled by two competing empires, and there was some sentiment amongst the people that it was best to be ruled by another Asian power instead of a Western power. Such sentiment was encouraged by the Japanese, who took a different approach to dealing with the local people on the peninsula over other regions they had invaded. Despite the kinds of hostility and cruelty exercised by the Japanese in other parts of the mainland, they seemed to make some efforts to show the Vietnamese people they would ultimately be treated better under Japanese control than they had been previously under the French. Not all Vietnamese people agreed with this idea, and this eventually created a significant divide within the nation, with no majority opinion on how best to move forward or what would be most beneficial for the Vietnamese people.

Following the Japanese invasion in 1940, the US paid more attention to the region. At the time, the US was not actively involved in World War II, but they were working to secure their interests in areas at war. America had not yet picked a side, but its relationship with France was much closer than with Japan. When the Japanese took control of Vietnam and the other parts of Indochina, the US moved to support the French administration. They established a military post in Kunming, located in the southern part of China.

This was the beginning of US involvement in the region, and it stretched beyond just establishing a presence. After the US joined the war, President Franklin Roosevelt started discussing the idea of helping Vietnam to establish its independence, ending not only the Japanese occupation but the French colonial period as well.

While Roosevelt was interested in supporting the Vietnamese, Ho Chi Minh's ideologies would have complicated the relationship. Ho Chi Minh followed the teachings of Vladimir Lenin, one of the founders of the Soviet Union, who also helped to lead the Bolshevik Revolution that ended the Russian monarchy. Ho Chi Minh used that inspiration to found the League for the Independence of Vietnam, better known as the Viet Minh. As the Japanese focused on their next move, Ho Chi Minh and his group began their work in May 1941, and the small band of communists continued to grow over the years of Japanese occupation. Ho Chi Minh even attempted to gain Chinese support, crossing the Chinese border to seek assistance for his cause. Unfortunately, the nationalist government arrested him, and when they eventually released him, Ho Chi Minh returned to Vietnam and worked with other Allied nations. He likely did not realize that the push for communism would undermine his efforts for independence. The US was helping him because the Japanese were clearly the greater threat. The US involvement with Ho Chi Minh had more to do with countering the efforts of Japan than with Vietnamese independence. The ideological differences were overlooked because it was politically expedient to partner with the Vietnamese against the Japanese.

Throughout the second world war, the US supported Ho Chi Minh and the Viet Minh resistance, as Ho Chi Minh was seen as "more nationalist than communist" and was, therefore, "an acceptable partner."[3] Not unlike the US's tenuous relationship with Russia to oppose German expansion, the US supported the communist Vietnamese group to counter Japanese incursion. Because of his efforts to oppose the Japanese, Ho Chi Minh was a convenient ally for the US. The Viet Minh provided intelligence on the Japanese military movements and organized resistance against the imperial force. With an established relationship with the growing superpower, Ho Chi Minh likely thought he might continue working with the US after the war to gain Vietnamese independence.[3]

In the early part of 1945, World War II was ending, and the Japanese recognized their situation was precarious. Deciding to end French control of Vietnam entirely and prevent any coordination between France and other Allied nations, the Japanese arrested French officials. Having done so, Japan gave control to Emperor Bao Dai, allowing him to declare Vietnam an independent country. Despite such a declaration, the region remained under Japanese control, and the Vietnamese government was little more than a puppet government.

The primary beneficiary of this shift in power was Ho Chi Minh. He did not openly battle with the Japanese because he knew they were retreating across Asia. He knew it was only a matter of time before the Allied nations returned, so he established a stronghold in a northern area of Vietnam that was not strategically important to the Japanese and who generally ignored it. From this marginal haven, Ho Chi Minh began establishing himself and the Viet Minh as the primary power. They recruited the local population into their cause, winning them over by helping during a food shortage. This earned them considerable goodwill, as Ho Chi Minh and his group were doing more to help the general population than any previous group had. As the Japanese continued to retreat, The Viet Minh spread farther south. By the time World War II ended, Vietnam was in a position to fight for control of its own nation.

The Cold War began not long after World War II. With most of the countries around the world not willing to engage in yet another disastrous war that would destroy property, land, lives, and economies, the world moved into a covert war, with two superpowers acting as the primary forces around the globe. The USSR promoted the spread of communism, sometimes by the use of force. This primarily happened in northern Europe when the USSR invaded and forced nations to join them. In the rest of the world, the USSR engaged in proxy wars and espionage instead of more direct fighting. The US was the primary driver in an attempt to spread democracy worldwide. In theory, this was not done by force. The US did not invade other nations, but they played a role in destabilizing nations in South America when it looked like communist leaders were gaining power.

Both nations spent a lot of money on wars around the world trying to defeat each other. Sometimes, they also provided military support, though it was more common for them to provide modern weaponry and strategists. Actual military engagement was avoided because of the threat of nuclear war. However, there were a few instances where the US, USSR, and China engaged in combat under the guise of supporting other nations, with Vietnam being one of the most detrimental examples of how costly these proxy wars could be.

THE EVENTS LEADING UP TO THE WAR

World War II prepared Vietnam for change, and the Viet Minh positioned themselves to be the local group advocating for independence when the war ended. The end of the Japanese occupation initially left questions about how the region would be governed, especially as France could not dedicate time and resources to reconstruction. Having been occupied by Germany for several years, the people of France were far more concerned with rebuilding their nation than helping their colonies.

With the Japanese occupiers removed, Ho Chi Minh also tried to break away from France. Having established a base of power in the north and slowly moving south as the Japanese retreated, he was in a much stronger position to take over the country to implement a government based on Lenin's ideas. On September 2, 1945, he made his intentions clear by declaring the nation's independence. Success would not only remove French control, but it would again differentiate the area as distinct from the other peninsular nations. Historically, the region was not a single entity but a group of several countries that did not always get along.

France rejected his declaration, setting up the region for another conflict. There was not as much fighting in this part of Asia as in many other regions (notably the nations closest to Japan). Compared to the fighting that had occurred elsewhere in Asia, Vietnam was spared from the same kinds of horrors. They were occupied by two nations on opposite sides of the war, and for most of the war, Japan and France struck a tentative balance of power. As World War 2 was now over and Japan removed from power, France was ready to restore the region as one of their colonies. With nations relying on resources from this region (the US relied on Vietnam for about half of their rubber use in the 1940s), France could have used the resources to help rebuild its own country, as well as improve their economy. When the French made it clear they were not going to leave, the Viet Minh began using the same guerilla tactics against the French they had used (with American support) against the Japanese.[4]

Immediately following the surrender of Japan, their puppet

leader, Emperor Bảo Đại abdicated.[5] This created a power vacuum in the country, and Minh moved into Hanoi to declare a new provisional government. Soon after, he declared the nation was independent, calling it the Democratic Republic of Vietnam. Following the example of the Bolshevik Revolution, he placed himself at the top of the power structure, but he called himself the president. Ho likely knew that the French would not simply give up on Vietnam and the other countries, so he worked to gain recognition for his country by the US. By this time, Roosevelt had died and President Harry Truman had replaced him. Truman was not like his predecessor, and Roosevelt had kept him in the dark about major decisions. Truman was unwilling to work with the communists in Vietnam, but he did not condemn Ho Chi Minh's work; he simply ignored him and the Viet Minh.

Both the Europeans and the Chinese sought to control the region, with the British sending troops to Saigon in South Vietnam and China sending forces to Hanoi in the north. The British freed the French personnel imprisoned by the Japanese, only for the newly released soldiers to turn on the Vietnamese people and massacre them, citing the justification that they were killing the Viet Minh. It was not just French soldiers who attacked Vietnamese men, women, and children; roughly 20,000 French civilians who lived in and around Saigon joined the tragic massacre. [6, 7]

The Viet Minh initiated their own atrocities—stopping commerce around the city and interrupting supplies of water and electricity. In the suburbs, the criminal organization Binh Xuyen, began massacring Europeans. Included in this massacre was one officer sent in to help the Viet Minh, OSS officer Lieutenant Colonel Peter Dewey. The Vietnamese thought he was a member of the French forces. Dewey had been reporting back to the US in the months leading up to his death, even warning those back home that the nation "ought to clear out of Southeast Asia."[8]

France sent a much larger force in October, pushing the Viet Minh out of Saigon. With the return of a more robust French force, China reached an agreement with the French to leave the northern part of Vietnam. In return, the French were to concede the use of ports in Shanghai and other parts of China back to the Chinese. In 1946, the French and the Viet Minh attempted to negotiate peace, although talks broke down fairly quickly and when Indochina's high commissioner declared a new government in the nation's south, fighting resumed.

In 1949, the Chinese Civil War finally ended, resulting in the rise of Mao Zedong and his party as the leaders of China. Truman and other American leaders saw this as a significant threat, leading to a dangerous foreign policy that sought to contain communism and keep it from spreading to other nations in Asia. [9] [10]

In 1950, the newly empowered People's Republic of China and the USSR recognized Ho Chi Minh's declaration of the Democratic Republic of Vietnam. Soon, China began sending them resources, including modern weapons made by the US, allowing the Viet Minh to form a more traditional type of military. In response, both the US and the UK recognized the government in the south run by Bao Dai but controlled by the French, with the US also sending money to support the French in the fight against the Viet Minh.

The war continued to rage across the nation, with fighters from both sides being funded and supplied by outside countries. Toward the end of 1953, the French sent in paratroopers near the Dien Bien Phu Valley, located near the nation's border with Laos. Fifteen-thousand French troops faced almost 50,000 Viet Minh led by General Vo Nguyen Giap. The location was essential to the Viet Minh as many of the supplies came from the border with Laos and the French planned to disrupt this supply line, diminishing the Viet Minh's ability to sustain fighting.

The French underestimated the Viet Minh, particularly General Giap, who was an exceptional strategist. Allowing the French to build up both a presence and their confidence, Giap and his troops bided their time until March 1954. Ready to act, they began a siege on the newly established outpost.

After nearly two months of fighting, the French finally surrendered. Over 2,000 of their troops were killed and roughly 11,000 were captured. According to the Viet Minh, they lost over 4,000 during the siege, but the French estimated their opponent's losses were likely closer to double that number.[11]

Following the Battle of Dien Bien Phu, both sides sought a peaceful solution through the 1954 Geneva Accords. The two regions signed the accords in July 1954, resulting in Vietnam being divided along the 17th parallel. Ho Chi Minh and his communist party were to control the northern part of the nation, while they officially placed the southern part of the nation under the control of Emperor Bao Dai. This was meant to be a short-term solution, with an election planned for two years after the agreement was signed, where a single leader would be elected, and the country would be reunified into one nation.

During those two years, the 17th parallel served as a way of dividing two different ideologies, but it was not nearly as straightforward as communism versus democracy. In reality, the Vietnamese really controlled neither part of the country, though Ho Chi Minh had more control than the USSR and China, who both supported him. The south clearly was not controlled by the Vietnamese but by a puppet government who was still theoretically under French control. Both sides of Vietnam were entrenched in their diverging ideologies, and different national identities formed, ever decreasing the likelihood of peaceful reunification.

At the same time, the US became increasingly involved in

the formation of the southern government, and President Ngo Dinh Diem further pressed for western ideas of what a government should be. By this point, there was a push in the south to be independent of French colonialism. While removing actual western control, they remained interested in the western European and North American governmental structure. The resulting government focused more on gaining power over the people, a change that led many of the people in South Vietnam to turn against this new style of government.

The election never happened. There was a fear that support for Ho Chi Minh, even in South Vietnam, would win him the election and place the entire country under communist rule. Without the chance to vote, an opportunity that many Vietnamese had waited for, resentment grew among the rest of the South Vietnamese, and war seemed inevitable.

JUSTIFICATION FOR US INVOLVEMENT IN VIETNAM

With the US policy to contain communism, the US was eager to ensure communism did not spread south of the 17th parallel. The policy failed to consider that no one was forcing communism on the south; the people in South Vietnam wanted to be ruled by Ho Chi Minh. He had so far helped to manage food supplies and minimize a famine following World War II while other countries were too busy with issues in their own homelands. Ho Chi Minh had proven himself dedicated to the people and not to his own power. He faced imprisonment in China for trying to win independence and fought the Japanese and French over two decades. This had won him the respect of people across Vietnam who had suffered and struggled under the six decades of French rule.

As predicted, when the election and promise of reunification agreed to by the Geneva Accords did not occur, hostilities resumed. Even though the local population in South Vietnam did not want to be under the rule of their government, the war was still split along the 17th parallel. By 1958, the war moved farther south, and the northern fighters started calling themselves the National Liberation Front or NLF. NLF forces were bolstered by those South Vietnamese who wanted to oust their own government in the south and pull the country back under one rule.

Although supported by the US, the southern prime minister, Diem, was seen as corrupt. Instead of winning over the people, he appeared more interested in replacing the French officials without changing much of the social structure. He refused to address the widening disparity between the wealthiest Vietnamese families and the peasants and continued to deny the peasants the rights to the land they worked on. Furthermore, as the leader of a nation where Buddhism was the primary religion, Diem, a Catholic himself, showed little recognition or respect for the faith of the people he governed.

According to President Dwight Eisenhower, the US supported Diem's refusal to hold the elections as the US feared the election would result in Vietnam becoming a communist country, not a democratic one. This was somewhat of a controversial stance, viewed by others as a subversive approach, and undermined the Vietnamese people's right to a free and fair election. Containment of communism had become the primary focus, despite being detrimental to the US's original objective, which was to encourage democracy.[12]

With an increasingly unpopular leader, South Vietnam grew at risk of falling to the communists. Without outside military intervention, it was all but certain the nation would be reunited under the communist rule of Ho Chi Minh. Vietnam choosing a communist government was not an acceptable result to the US leaders.

In November 1963, Diem and his brother were assassinated by members of their own military. That same month, President

John F. Kennedy was assassinated in the US. Both events created great unrest in South Vietnam and the US. While the US quickly inaugurated President Lyndon Johnson, the South Vietnamese government was thrown into disarray and there was no strong contender to assume control of the government immediately.

2

THE SKY SOLDIERS ENTER VIETNAM

American soldiers had been in Vietnam since 1954, though their role had changed many times. Throughout the 1950s, soldiers were tasked with training South Vietnamese soldiers to fight with updated, more modern tactics. What had started as just over 350 advisors in 1954 had grown into a small military force of 23,000 by the beginning of 1965. The US had been preparing to assist Vietnam well before action was approved. By the time Congress officially approved military action in the region, the lines between "advisor" and "combatant" had long been blurred for those military personnel already in Vietnam.[1]

The Johnson administration began a bombing campaign in March 1965. The bombing campaign was called Operation ROLLING THUNDER, and it was intended to frustrate the North Vietnamese communists and reduce their ability to fight[2] while also boosting the morale of the US-aligned fighting force of Vietnam, the Army of the Republic of Vietnam (ARVN), which was garrisoned in Saigon.

While Operation ROLLING THUNDER could achieve some of its goals, the operation was unable to deter the North Vietnamese fighting forces, the People's Army of Vietnam (PAVN), and the nontraditional guerrilla army known as the VC to cease its campaign against the South Vietnamese.[3] Soon, the bombing campaign would lead to troops on the ground. Once those troops on the ground were committed, the war escalated quickly. "By the end of 1965, 185,000 US troops were in Vietnam. The number peaked in 1968 at nearly 550,000. Over 2.6 million servicemen and women eventually served in Vietnam."[1] One of the first units mobilized was a small unit already stationed in Asia.

The 173rd Airborne Brigade was a recently reactivated unit, having initially formed around the time the US became involved in World War I and reactivated in Okinawa in 1963. The Chinese soldiers were the ones who gave them their nickname, calling the soldiers "Tien Bien," which translates roughly to "sky soldiers." Apparently, they had left an impression on the nationalist Chinese paratroopers. The name stuck and persists to this day.[4]

When the US was ready to escalate from a bombing campaign to one that involved troops on the ground, the 173rd Brigade was the obvious choice. Not only were they pre-positioned in the same geographic region as Vietnam, they had been training in jungles similar to those in Vietnam, and there was an expectation that paratroopers might be an important aspect of winning the war.

> "When Johnson gave his OK to introduce US Army combat troops to Vietnam, the 173rd Airborne Brigade was the first to go, ordered to provide security for Bien Hoa Air Base, twelve miles northeast of Saigon. Stationed in Okinawa, Japan, the 173rd Airborne was the Pacific area's 'fire brigade,' prepared to respond to any crises in the region."[5]

It became the first major unit sent to Vietnam at the beginning of the war and the first US Army ground combat unit committed to operations. The Unit was 10% under strength, however, and they were given the difficult task of protecting Bien Hoa Air Base, which was located not far from Saigon and which faced a troublesome area called War Zone D. Whilst the 173rd Airborne had participated in various wars going back to the first world war, this conflict differed in tactics from previous operations and the Sky Soldiers would quickly have to learn how to fight this new kind of war.[6]

HISTORY OF THE 173RD AIRBORNE BRIGADE

The 173rd Airborne Brigade was originally created as the US prepared to enter World War I in 1917 as the 173rd Infantry Brigade. The concept of the Airborne Brigade did not exist then, as we know it today. There had been some military skirmishes and problems since the American Civil War, but the US had not been engaged in any serious conflict since that war ended in 1865. The American Civil War also significantly changed the American military, so creating new troops, brigades, platoons, and other military groups was necessary before the US could engage in a war that came to be known as a world war. Initially, the 173rd was meant to be an infantry group that would join the 87th Division to fight in France. Following the end of World War I, the brigade returned to the US in 1919 and was demobilized and reorganized several times over the following two decades into the Headquarters and Headquarters Company (HHC) 173rd Infantry Brigade.

Roughly two decades later, as Europe and Asia became embroiled in yet another conflict, Americans viewed the outbreak of World War II with skepticism and wariness. They felt the justification for World War I had not been worth the loss of life and many Americans were unwilling to engage in more fighting. However, following the attack on Pearl Harbor in December 1942, Americans were finally persuaded they needed to act before the Axis Powers crushed the nations who were fighting against them.

US forces were reorganized before entering World War II and brigades were eliminated from divisions. Consequently, the HHC 173rd Infantry Brigade was redesignated as the 87th Reconnaissance Troop in February 1942 and under this banner, maintained the 173rd's lineage throughout World War II. After returning to Alabama from Europe at the end of the war, the troop was eventually inactivated on December 1, 1951.

As the world moved on from World War II and into the Cold War, several major incidents and events set the US on edge. As the US prepared itself for future conflict, the 173rd Airborne Brigade was activated in 1963 and chartered to serve as the quick reaction force for Pacific Command.[7]

The brigade comprised the following:

- The 1st to 4th Battalions
- Company D, 16th Armor
- Troop E, 17th Cavalry
- The 3rd Battalion, 319th Airborne Artillery
- 335th Aviation Company

More forces from other units would later join them, namely:

- The 4th Battalion, 503rd Infantry from Fort Campbell in June 1966
- The 3rd Battalion, 503rd Infantry in September 1967[8]

The Sky Soldiers were the first major unit in the US Army to join the war effort in Vietnam as a specialized force. They eventually served in Vietnam for six years, engaging in active combat throughout.

As the soldiers headed to war, for many of them, it was the first time they faced actual combat, unaware that the military advisors already in Vietnam had recommended the withdrawal of US troops from the country as the situation deteriorated. Aside from tales told by fellow soldiers as they passed through the Sky Soldiers' base in Okinawa, very few Americans knew the whole truth about what was happening in the country. The Sky Soldiers entered the war with little idea of what awaited them. Despite their strategic advantage, superior firepower, and a strong sense of duty, the Sky Soldiers faced a fighting force in the VC who felt they were defending their country from foreign empires and were willing to engage in brutal guerrilla warfare tactics. The North Vietnamese saw the Americans as no different from the French or the Japanese, as foreigners interfering in the transfer of power in Vietnam, yet the Sky Soldiers were led to believe they were helping the people of South Vietnam defend themselves in a brutal civil war. This perception was likely in stark contrast to the way many Vietnamese felt about the change in leadership, and proved to be incredibly problematic for American troops as war began to rage.

Upon their arrival in Vietnam, the Sky Soldiers' primary focus was on protecting Bien Hoa Air Base and ensuring the northern forces weren't able to compromise the city of Saigon or the Saigon-Bien Hoa complex. Saigon is close to the Vietnamese border with Cambodia, and there was already a sizable force of communist fighters near the area.

By the time US troops arrived in the area, the US had divided the southern region of Vietnam into four tactical regions:

- I Corps–The northernmost region with the most fighting and loss of life. They primarily stationed American Marines in this area.
- II Corps–This area included the nation's Central Highlands and Dak To and was where Americans initially were able to push their opponents into Cambodia and Laos.
- III Corps–This included Saigon and was the primary location for American Army soldiers. Their primary focus was to keep the VC from advancing from their camps and gaining new territory. Initially, this was where the US focused its attention to ensure the VC did not establish a presence that would threaten the densely populated region.
- IV Corps–The group known as the Brown Water Navy took up patrols in the rivers and other main bodies of water in the southernmost part of southern Vietnam. Their patrols focused on the waterways associated with the Mekong Delta.[9]

These tactical areas were further divided into smaller regions to focus on different types of attacks. Commanders sent the Sky Soldiers to III Corps, a region known as War Zone D, which included the lands around the Dong Nai River north of Bien Hoa. The VC had created a base there allowing them to infiltrate into other regions in the southern part of the country. This threat was dangerous for the American military since it put the enemy much farther into South Vietnam.

War Zone D was a fairly small region to the east of the III

Corps and bordered II Corps. Roughly 10km north of the city of Bien Hoa, the war zone incorporated parts of several provinces, including Phuoc Long, Long Khanh, Binh Duong, and Bien Hoa. Several routes mostly outlined War Zone D, making it easier to identify where to send supplies and soldiers. Along the north of the war zone was Route 14, while Route 13 ran along the western side. The Dong Nai River marked the boundaries along both the eastern and southern boundaries of the zone.

At the beginning of US involvement in the war, much of the fighting took place in War Zone D as the US wanted to neutralize the VC based near large population centers. The Sky Soldiers played a vital role during the early days of American involvement, especially in attempting to destroy the VC strong-holds in the area. Their immense impact on the war would be felt due to three operations in particular: Operation HUMP, Operation MARAUDER, and Operation CRIMP, all of which will be explored in the following chapter.

WAR ZONE D OPERATIONS

The key focus for US commanders was to deny the communists freedom of movement in the south; they never intended to conquer the north. There was not a plan to unseat Ho Chi Minh or to disrupt his efforts to rule over the people in North Vietnam. As a result, most of the fighting occurred in the southern strategic areas where the VC had gained ground; the strategic focus was on removing them. US forces executed large operations in the locality during the first few years to fulfill this initial goal.

It is difficult to overstate the significance of the Sky Soldiers' efforts during these large operations and early battles of the US forces against the VC. Initially, the northern troops were far better supplied than the Americans thought they were. Unlike the Americans, the VC also had a distinct advantage because they were very familiar with the local geography. The Americans were poorly acclimatized and ill adapted to jungle warfare, and the tactical edge sat with the VC and their infamous booby traps.

The US strategists and politicians had wholly underestimated the VC, and it was the troops on the ground who bore the detrimental impact of this intelligence failure. Coupled with a lack of strategic direction, American soldiers faced many unexpected challenges, and the path to victory remained unclear.

The Sky Soldiers were among some of the first to fight the VC, and they quickly learned that the war they were engaged in was nothing like the stories they had heard from their parents and grandparents about prior American military engagements. There were few similarities between the wars during the first half of the century compared to those that came in the second half. Yet the brigade won some early successes to bolster morale and esprit de corps during the first couple of years.

OPERATION HUMP

America was not the only nation concerned about what might happen in Vietnam after the French left. The Australian government also monitored the situation and wanted to prevent communism from spreading further south. Soldiers from both countries prepared to work together to fight the VC, with the American 1st Battalion, 503rd Infantry Regiment, 173rd Airborne Brigade and the Australian 1st Battalion, Royal Australian Regiment being the primary forces during the first major operation.

Up to this point, American soldiers had only experienced skirmishes and short conflicts with the VC. These soldiers had joined the military by choice (the US did not start drafting soldiers until December 1, 1969), so they had been trained extensively and were aware of standard fighting strategies. The initial deployment was for twelve months, so as the soldiers prepared for this first big operation, they fully expected to be returning home over the next six months if they survived the fighting.

When the strategists could finally prepare for a more sustained engagement, the American soldiers thought they were at the back end of their deployment. The operation was coming after they had cleared the "hump" of their deployment, thus telling us something about how the soldiers were feeling at the time. They perceived Operation HUMP similarly as office workers perceive Wednesdays—a "Hump Day," when the work week is half over. In theory, Operation HUMP was supposed to be the homeward stretch for the Sky Soldiers. Unfortunately, this was the beginning of a significant increase in active fighting, which continued for the next year.[1]

Until this point, there was good reason for American soldiers to think the operation would be successful and perhaps even an easy victory. The minor skirmishes and clashes thus far ended with the VC fleeing from the area. The North Vietnamese soldiers seemed in perpetual retreat, giving the Americans a false sense of certainty about what to expect during this much longer and more aggressive push to remove the northern fighters.

Despite numerous successful clashes with the VC, the Sky Soldiers remained unfamiliar with their doctrine and tactics. The northern forces controlled several tactically advantageous hills in the region and the US strategists wanted to remove them since they located enemy only about 17.5 miles from Bien Hoa. The American 1st Battalion, 173rd Airborne Brigade, and 503rd Infantry Regiment were sent northwest of the Song Be River and Dong Nai River, where they mounted a helicopter assault on the VC position. The 1st Battalion Royal Australian Regiment headed south of Dong Nai to conduct an assault. Late on November 7, 1965, the American forces established themselves near their target, Hill 65, and both B and C Companies of the 503rd set up defensive positions during the night in the thick jungle near the hill.

The joint assault began on November 8, 1965, and the allied forces came face-to-face with the VC on the first morning. The VC initiated their own ambush of the 1st Battalion C Company, as they made their way toward Hill 65. Suddenly, facing a much more brutal fight than they had previously experienced, C Company was in significant danger, as they found themselves outnumbered nearly six to one. The VC isolated some soldiers, causing B Company to work their way toward the larger enemy group to help the embattled company. As B Company moved forward, the fighting became increasingly ferocious, forcing the soldiers to use bayonets at close range. The VC soldiers were well aware of how superior the American military was, especially in terms of air strikes and artillery, so they hoped to remove most of the Sky Soldiers' advantages by keeping the fighting in close quarters. The VC's tactic was to draw the Sky Soldiers into close combat before quickly fleeing.

"Staying close to or 'hugging' American units in battle (also known as 'grabbing or clinging to the enemy's belt'), a tactic the Viet Minh employed in the First Indochina War, was arguably one of the most effective.

Gen. Nguyen Chi Thanh formalized the use of 'hugging' tactics while serving as party secretary of the communist Central Office for South Vietnam (COSVN) in 1965. Thanh, upon learning that a squad leader in a VC main-force regiment had shouted, 'Grab the enemy's belts to fight them,' while fighting the South Vietnamese, ordered all communist units to adopt the rallying cry as a slogan when fighting US forces."[2]

When it became clear they needed more assistance to reach C Company, B Company launched artillery strikes toward the largest clusters of VC, hoping to drive them back quickly so they could reach C Company. This seemed to work the way they wanted it to initially as the VC appeared to stop fighting. Unfortunately for the American soldiers, the VC commander sent troops around to outflank B Company, pressing in on their area. Seeing an opportunity to get C Company to safety, American soldiers began retrieving the bodies of their fallen comrades and assisting the injured to a place where they could be treated. Other soldiers were preparing for a longer battle as it became clear their opponents did not want to be pushed out of their current locations. While watching the Sky Soldiers work to assist their own and prepare for more fighting, the VC commander thought his men could cut the US soldiers off from calling for more reinforcements or air strikes. If the commander had been right, this would have given his troops a distinct advantage.

Despite the VC's best efforts, though, the soldiers of the 503rd fought in hand-to-hand combat while rescuing their soldiers. One particular soldier played a vital role in assisting those who had fallen and required medical attention—Specialist Fifth Class Lawrence Joel. He was a part of the 1st Airborne Battalion, 503rd Infantry, 173rd Airborne Brigade. He received a bullet wound to his leg fairly early in the operation, but he did not stop working to bring injured soldiers back for medical attention. He moved through the fallen soldiers to find those who were still alive and needed help. During one of his skirmishes, he was hit a second time in his thigh, but he still did not stop making his way through the enemy fire to help his fellow soldiers. He treated thirteen more soldiers following his second injury. Until the evacuation began on the 9th, he did not stop tending to the wounded and comforting those who were not likely to make it. Upon his return to the US, he gained recognition from his fellow soldiers and military leaders. Eventually, President Johnson heard of his efforts and, in March 1967, awarded this outstanding soldier with a Congressional Medal of Honor. During the ceremony on the lawn of the White House, Johnson said that Joel had shown "a very special kind of courage—the unarmed heroism of compassion and service to others." Joel became the first medic who fought in Vietnam to earn the Medal of Honor, and he was the first African American who was still alive to receive the medal since the 1898 Spanish-

American War. His hometown recognized him by naming a coliseum after him: Lawrence Joel Veterans Memorial Coliseum.

Eventually, US and Australian forces were able to push the VC out of the area and take Hill 65. Early the next day, an evacuation began. The 503rd lost forty-nine soldiers, and significantly more were wounded. The 1st Battalion, Royal Australian Regiment lost two men during their part of the operation, as well as several injured. Operation HUMP was considered a success, but it came at a high cost to the 173rd Brigade. It remains one of the brigade's most deadly encounters throughout its history.

OPERATION MARAUDER

For most of their time in Vietnam, commanders stationed the Sky Soldiers near the Bien Hoa Air Force Base. The term loosely translates to "land of peaceful frontiers," and the Sky Soldiers hoped to return the area to its previous peacefulness. Following the success of the first operation, the Sky Soldiers had almost a month with fewer fierce engagements but at the end of December 1965, they were tasked with finding and removing the VC from Bao Trai located in the Mekong Delta. By this time, the VC's 506th Battalion had been established in the region for over a year, so they were no longer monitoring forces inside South Vietnam. Intelligence also reported that the 267th VC Main Force Battalion was traveling through the region. Attacking them would be unexpected since the VC in this area had largely been left alone.

Following Operation HUMP, nearly two months passed before the Sky Soldiers engaged in another major operation. Their second operation was on another significant day—New Year's Day, 1966. Known as Operation MARAUDER, this second effort was another joint operation that included US, Australian, and New Zealand forces. The 173rd was not the only fighting force with a catchy nickname; the Australians sported the moniker "the Diggers" and the New Zealand soldiers were referred to as "Kiwis."

The 'Plain of Reeds' was the name given to the area roughly thirty-five miles west of Saigon and was close to the Bao Trai airfield. It frequently proved to be a place where forces organized their soldiers since it had been a base for resistance fighters during the first and second Indochina Wars. The VC were incredibly familiar with the location because of its constant use over the last few decades. Operation MARAUDER would be the first time US forces would launch an operation in the area.[3]

ESTABLISHING AREAS AND DIVIDING THE UNITS

Brigadier General Ellis Williamson was in command of the American forces in the area, and he was one of the driving forces behind Operation MARAUDER. Likely aware of the significance of the VC's presence and the potential to remove them from an established position near the most populated parts of the country, he wanted to create a command post that could help remove the VC from the Plain of Reeds. The US 1st Battalion was supposed to be dropped near the Vam Co Dong River to look for the VC to the west. The Australian 1st Battalion was to be dropped east of the river to disrupt or destroy operations in the northeastern area. The American 2nd Battalion, 503rd Infantry was to be moved to the Brigade Base at Bao Trai, then would either move to reinforce the US 1st Battalion or the Australian forces, whichever one encountered the most significant enemy contact.

The different landing zones, known as LZ, were each identified by a different type of alcoholic beverage:

- The Brigade Base at Bao Trai was called LZ Whiskey.
  All divisions were to transit through LZ Whiskey
  before further deploying to their respective LZs.

- The area west of the Vam Co Dong River was called LZ Vodka. On January 1, 1966, the US 1st Battalion, led by Lieutenant Colonel John Tyler, was helilifted to this area.
- The area east of the river was called LZ Scotch. On January 1, 1966, the Australian Battalion, led by Lieutenant Colonel Alex Preece, was helilifted to this area.[4]
- The area to the south was called LZ Wine. On January 2, 1966, the US 2nd Battalion, led by Lieutenant Colonel George Dexter, was helilifted to this area.

January 1 and 2, 1966

Operation MARAUDER began on January 1, 1966. The first day saw minimal fighting as troops established the base quickly at Bao Trai with no significant problems and no encounters with the VC. Shortly after noon on the first day of the operation, the US 1st Battalion was dropped at LZ Vodka, where they encountered little resistance for the first couple of hours as they swept through the Plain of Reeds. After a few more hours, B Company came into contact with a few dozen VC close to the river. The VC were armed enough to put up some resistance, leading to the wounding of three members of B Company. The fighting did not intensify because the supporting airstrikes and artillery pushed the VC back after roughly an hour of fighting.

Later that same day, the Australian Battalion was dropped at LZ Whiskey as the US 503rd was taken to their destination. Later that afternoon, the helicopters returned to LZ Whiskey to take the Australian battalion to their next destination, LZ Scotch. They were dropped near Can Thuy, a larger village near the river. Though they were fortunate enough to have very little resistance or encounters with the enemy, they noted the locations of many enemy bunkers that were not occupied.

As the different units submitted their reports, it became clear why they had not encountered many VC. The fields were flooded, which the VC would likely have expected given the time of year and their familiarity with the region. The region is a river delta, so there are many streams, creeks, and other small bodies of water all over the area. Complicating matters was a system of dikes that ran parallel to the river, many of which obscured bunkers full of VC combatants. With widespread flooding and the obscured bunkers, it became difficult to move through the fields because all the small bodies of water had overrun their banks.

As the units out in the field slowly progressed through the water-logged areas, the US 2nd Battalion stayed at their location in Bao Trai on January 1, which is where all supporting artillery and airstrikes would be launched from. On January 2, 1966, when it became apparent the 2nd Battalion would not be needed to reinforce either of the units already in the field, they relocated to LZ Wine. Lieutenant Colonel Dexter moved A and B Company along the southwest, then headed northwest until they met with the Australian Battalion.

Suspecting there might be more VC near LZ Wine, Colonel Dexter called in supporting fire to drive away any guerrilla fighters in the field; this included artillery fire and helicopter gunships. As the gunships left the area where the soldiers were to be dropped, they were met with far more enemy fire than any of the other forces encountered during the operation. Knowing it could be potentially disastrous to drop his troops so close to a larger opposition force, Colonel Dexter moved the drop-off point roughly 500 meters to the northwest.

US B Company was the first group of troops to be taken into the field that day. They landed in sugar cane fields and began making their way to LZ Wine. As Colonel Dexter had expected, they began encountering VC to their front and to their left flank. As they made their way to the LZ, more VC formed along their left flank. By the time A Company arrived, the fighting had increased. The VC began firing on the helicopters, killing a gunner in one door of the helicopter and injuring several soldiers as they exited the aircraft. Once the soldiers of B Company were on the ground, the VC quickly pinned down both American companies. The location where the two companies were supposed to meet had a machine gun protected by a concrete bunker. With B Company exposed on their flank, the machine gun could harm the company significantly, resulting in heavy casualties. To make matters worse, they were dealing with friendly fire as shells from supporting aircraft landed on B Company. The commander of B Company lacked the experience necessary to get B Company out of their predicament, and the mud of the flooded area bogged down A Company, preventing them from providing support.

A Company tried to take another route to reach B Company, encountering heavy fire. Unable to make any progress, A Company soldiers began looking for any kind of cover available in an open field. A Company commander, Captain Carmen Cavezza, tried to order artillery support for his troops, but it did not arrive for several hours and when it did, the soldiers had to work in a way that left them vulnerably launching mortars out in the open.

Another casualty of the chaos near LZ Wine was a US Air Force pilot who flew his Cessna low and close to the fighting, unfortunately putting him in the way of American artillery. One of the rounds launched by the Americans struck the aircraft and the pilot died on impact. The operation was turning into a disaster.

Colonel Dexter sent two of the three C Company platoons and D Company into the fray at 1030 hours to support the pinned-down A and B Companies. He intended for them to head southwest, moving around A Company's current location, where they would outflank the VC. Since this unit had armored vehicles, they had a difficult time moving through the mud and became bogged down in the fields, but they pushed forward, intent on providing much-needed support to their fellow soldiers. With D Company unable to move forward, C Company moved slowly forward without them, finally reaching A Company later in the afternoon. A Company had spent roughly eight hours primarily stuck in one location looking for a way forward.

At 1600 hours, the two platoons reached their destination. With reinforcements bolstering their numbers, Colonel Dexter ordered them to head southwest to attack the VC more aggressively. This sparked the worst firefight of the operation so far.

Five members of A Company helped to change the trajectory of the battle as they overran the VC, who were adjacent to the machine gun bunker. With this threat removed, A Company began working down the dike where many bunkers were housed, sending the VC running. Soon afterwards, A Company broke through the VC's defenses. During this fight, Cavezza was shot in the stomach. Knowing he could not continue to command his troops effectively, he put Lieutenant Linn Lancaster in charge of A Company. After directing Lancaster to take charge, Cavezza told him, "Win this battle first, then evacuate the casualties."[4] Those were his last words before he passed out from his wounds. Luckily, Cavezza survived and his account is one of the main sources of information about the battle.

As A Company broke the VC's battalion, the VC troops began running in many directions, which is the typical way guerilla fighters operate. Many of these soldiers ended up running into the areas where B and C Companies were trying to conduct their sweeps. Since they were working through heavily water-logged areas, one trooper, Sergeant Charles Brown of B Company, quipped, "This is the first time I gave infantry hand signals under water, like hey fellas, swim over this way."

Survivors of this battle later recalled losing soldiers they had been talking to just days earlier. Soldiers were being shot as they tried to run toward different areas and out of the line of fire. Some died instantaneously, while others were injured and could not keep running. One soldier remembered calling for a medic after watching one soldier running beside him get shot between the eyes and another in the head. The second soldier was still alive, so the specialist who saw him fall called out for a medic to help him before moving forward to continue the attack. As the Americans approached, the VC, who had been in a position on one of the dikes, fled. It is unknown how many VC survived, but when the Americans reached the area where they had been positioned, there were ninety-eight VC who had been killed, six who were injured, and a vast amount of abandoned equipment.

The dike, where the VC had largely held their position for most of the day, was finally cleared and the three companies could finally meet up, although they were forced to rest on the dike overnight. One specialist later remembered how difficult it was to sleep there as he was "awakened by people cussing, as the troopers rolled off the dike and into the water while they were sleeping."[4]

Initially, Colonel Dexter had tentatively planned to order a night attack toward the southwest; however, the three companies had accomplished more than expected on January 2 and so he allowed the men to rest after such a difficult day. Several other factors went into his decision not to follow the fleeing VC. Not only did he have inexperienced commanders running two of the three companies, the soldiers were exhausted after fighting both the VC and the environment. They had broken the defenses of the 267th VC Main Force Battalion, but as night fell, Dexter had no idea where the 506th Local Force was located. Finally, the fighting had been so much worse than anticipated and they had used up all their reinforcements.

The US 1st Battalion had been active on January 2, but they encountered very little resistance. They found a tunnel system that could have resulted in a similar situation to the one the US 2nd Battalion faced, but the tunnel system in and around LZ Vodka was empty.

Similarly, the Diggers swept the area around LZ Scotch, occasionally encountering VC. They encountered one particularly difficult VC fighter, though, whom they identified as "H&I Charlie." H&I stood for Harassment and Interdiction fire, and Charlie was the name Allied soldiers gave to VC fighters. This particular fighter had a Thompson submachine gun and was clearly very familiar with the region. Australian Colonel Bob Breen later recalled how this one fighter constantly pinned down members of the Australian battalion. "He would pop up, fire, disappear under water, and reappear later in a different place."[4] After he had done this repeatedly, one captain ordered an armored personnel carrier to wait in the water for him to emerge. When he did, the machine gunner killed the VC fighter.

January 3, 1966

Shortly after midnight on January 3, 1966, the 2nd Battalion began attacking toward the southwest. As they progressed, Sergeant Jerry Morton of C Company called for "fire for effect" mortars on a suspected enemy position. As C Company watched the round going over them, Morton realized something was wrong, and he began shouting into his radio to cease fire. Two of the mortars landed amid C Company, killing Morton and nineteen-year-old Private First Class George Geoghagen. One mortar injured eight other soldiers. Specialist Vester Reid was one of the wounded, having been thrown backward by the blast and sustaining serious stomach injuries. Jerry Levy, a combat medic, lost part of his leg and was also bleeding profusely in the groin area. Despite this, he dragged himself back to Specialist Reid and the other soldiers to save them.

Before Levy could tend to his own wounds, he sadly succumbed to them.[4]

The mortars had been launched from the Kiwi 161-gun battery. Horrified by the friendly fire, the commander of the gun battery, Major Don Kenning, checked the data on the weapons they used. It became tragically clear that the wet environment had made the propellant damp, causing less combustion and the rounds to fall short.

Word quickly got back to Colonel Dexter about the incident and that one commander, Captain Henchell, was injured in the friendly fire. He issued an order to Henchell's replacement, Colonel Thomas Faley, to take over and immediately evacuate all the casualties. Once they were cleared, C Company was to be reorganized, and the attack was to continue. Soon Faley was heading to meet the remaining members of the C Company commanders. He made his way slowly toward them, constantly bogged down by the mud, water, and heavy VC fire. Upon arriving to assume command of C Company, he debriefed with Henchell as medics were treating the injured officer. Once Faley had the details, he ordered the evacuation of the casualties, starting with those with the most serious wounds.

As the evacuation started, the VC opened fire on the medevacs (medical evacuations). Specialist Reid survived the initial blast, and as he was being taken out on a stretcher, the VC shot his leg, breaking both bones below the knee. Faley called in another platoon to attack the VC from a different angle to keep them occupied during the medevac.

While C Company was being treated, evacuated, and reorganized, the other two companies continued to push forward. By the end of the day, the VC had fled, leaving the Vam Co Dong banks clear for the US 2nd Battalion to create a perimeter as the day turned into night on January 3. With skirmishes winding down, leaders began restocking their weapons and analyzing the casualties. In thirty-six hours, sixteen soldiers died, and another sixty-seven were injured as a result of both fighting the VC and friendly fire.

January 4 to 8, 1966

January 4, 1966, saw very little enemy contact by any of the units. The US 2nd Battalion organized patrols to monitor the perimeter established the previous evening. For the first time since they had been sent into the fields, they had very little activity. As January 5, 1966, began, Staff Sergeant Leroy Davis was digging out an area to establish a better position to defend the soldiers at night. Before the patrol left for the day, Davis found a cache of weapons, including a Browning automatic rifle and some books with data about the VC. They placed everything in waterproof plastic to keep it safe from the environment. As the soldiers went out for their patrol, Colonel Dexter called in mine detectors to see if there were other caches within the perimeter. By the end of the day, they found many weapons and munitions without having to leave their established area.

On January 6, patrols were going out looking for caches. When they neared Ap Xuan Khanh, they found the 506th Local Force Battalion's headquarters. It was abandoned. The area around the headquarters had many mines and booby traps, so a demolition and mine detection team was called in to clear out the dangers. In addition to six automatic weapons, a large stash of ammunition, and 400 grenades, the teams found over 7,000 VC documents, including rosters, training documents, and maps.

Since they had not been heavily engaged in fighting, US 1st Battalion instead captured people they suspected of being VC and asked local residents about the location of the 506th Local Force Battalion. The local people told the soldiers the VC had been working in the area for a long time, but that they had been slowly breaking away into small groups and leaving the area around the time the Sky Soldiers, Diggers, and Kiwis arrived.

The Diggers had been doing similar work, patrolling the area they had secured. They found one large ammunition cache and several food caches. On January 5, they encountered a VC platoon near Hoa Khanh, but the platoon quickly fled.

ENDING OPERATION MARAUDER

A little over a week after Operation MARAUDER began, it ceased. Allied forces were able to secure the area by January 8, 1966, and had not seen any significant battles since January 2, 1966. Perhaps more importantly, a decisive blow was struck against the VC 267th Main Force Battalion. It rendered the enemy unit inoperative for the foreseeable future and the 173rd had a major victory to boost morale. They were met with adversity early in the fighting and overcame it, proving themselves to be a dangerous enemy to the VC forces. As Operation MARAUDER came to an end, the Sky Soldiers, Diggers, and Kiwis prepared for the next major initiative.

OPERATION CRIMP

Following the enemy findings of Operation MARAUDER on January 6, 1966, the three nations realized that search- and-destroy missions could yield much greater success. Although Operation MARAUDER was only just ending, military leaders launched the third major operation on January 7, 1966, called Operation CRIMP. The plan was to conduct a similar search-and-destroy plan roughly twenty-five miles northwest of Saigon. Like Operation MARAUDER, commanders wanted to remove all major VC headquarters and associated forces in the area and then secure it.[5]

Since the troops were still engaged on Operation

MARAUDER, commanders deployed a further 8,000 soldiers to this second region to secure it. Sky Soldiers, Diggers, and Kiwis again worked together to clear the region of the guerilla fighters. The US also provided aerial support, including the use of B-52 Stratofortress strategic bombers.

The ground differed significantly from the wet region of the delta. This region had some open areas where rubber plantations had been abandoned by the VC and people who fled from the fighting. The Ho Bo Woods was located in this region, making for engagements in the jungle. The fighting in this region was sporadic, but the VC had set up far more booby traps and hidden mines all around the region before they fled.

The Diggers encountered the fiercest firefights and they were heavily engaged with the VC during a long battle on the afternoon of January 8. They fought for the rest of the day, but when the Diggers prepared to fight the next morning, the VC soldiers were gone. As the Diggers swept through the location where the communists had been, the Australians found a large, impressive underground base, which was clearly the reason the VC had fought so hard during the previous afternoon. Not only did the headquarters have a complicated set of tunnels stretching out underground, but it was also a complex facility. Besides barracks and storage spaces, there were kitchens and medical facilities that ensured the VC could live underground. The Allied force began to realize, these underground tunnel systems allowed the VC to escape their strongholds without being seen.

As the Sky Soldiers, Diggers and Kiwis continued to move through the region, the soldiers found the same kind of extensive tunnel systems, although most were abandoned. In the headquarters cleared by the Australians, soldiers found a tremendous amount of data and documents concerning VC intentions, including one notebook that belonged to a senior political officer. This notebook became one of the most important intelligence findings of the entire war, along with a further 7,500 documents found in the extensive tunnel systems.

The soldiers began their sweep on January 8, and the operation ended on January 14, 1966. The Allied western forces had lost twenty-three soldiers, primarily Australians, and 102 soldiers were wounded, with booby traps and mines being the primary cause for these casualties.

The most important lesson learned from Operation CRIMP was the discovery of the tunnel systems used by the VC to escape, meaning US forces would need a new strategy to secure regions in War Zone D and other areas as the war continued.

Whilst these initial operations were strategic victories and led to some very useful intelligence gathering, they also highlighted there was still a great deal that allied western forces did not know about their foe. Taking what they had learned so far, US forces began planning their next move: a large-scale airborne operation named Operation JUNCTION CITY.

OPERATIONS CEDAR FALLS AND JUNCTION CITY

The initial operations in War Zone D were considered successful. There had been some significant fighting, but it never lasted more than a couple of days. With War Zone D finally secured, the western military leaders turned their attention to War Zone C. They started making plans to initiate a more effective and efficient operation that would push the VC out much faster. Knowing the opposition had tunnels that would allow them to easily leave battlefields unseen meant the war could go on indefinitely. The Allied commanders hoped to devise a strategy that would cripple the VC and provide the western forces with a significant win, perhaps causing the VC to rethink returning to the area.

Based on what they learned from the earlier search-and-destroy operations, military strategists devised one of the most instrumental operations of the Vietnam War: Operation JUNCTION CITY.[1] The aim of the near three-month operation was to locate the elusive command center of the communist uprising, thought to be located in War Zone C. The strategists also sought to ensure the VC did not have adequate time to escape the assault by taking the communist forces completely by surprise and overwhelming them, giving them no time to flee.

OPERATION CEDAR FALLS

A year passed between the end of Operation CRIMP and the next major operation, Operation CEDAR FALLS. During this time, the Sky Soldiers continued at their headquarters in Bien whilst also maintaining a presence across the four provinces surrounding Saigon. This ensured the VC still operating in War Zone D did not reestablish themselves near to the major city from an area where they previously had nearly unfettered movements. The Sky Soldiers predominantly moved around Long Khanh, Phuoc Long, Phuoc Tuy, and Xuan Loc between January 1966 and early February 1967. Occasionally, they were sent to the Central Highlands located in Pleiku and Kontum, where they regularly encountered VC.

During this period, the worst fighting occurred in a region called the Iron Triangle. It covered roughly 120 square miles in the Binh Duong Province and it was a place where the Viet Minh established a stronghold when fighting the French in the 1940s.[2] The VC were the natural successors from that period but now they were fighting other western forces and the US-aligned South Vietnamese government. The region included the Saigon River along the south, giving the VC several means of quickly leaving the area and returning later.

US and Australian forces planned and organized Operation CEDAR FALLS to remove the VC using the "hammer-and-anvil" strategy. In the first week of 1967, strategists stationed forces up and down the Saigon River. A large unit of the armored cavalry and the airborne units were to cut through the area after it had been mostly stripped of its vegetation, forcing the VC forces into the units and blocking their escape. Efforts were made to remove civilians from the area so they would not be trapped in what was to become the biggest operation up to this point.

One of the first moves made by the Allied western forces pressing the VC toward the blocking forces was to capture the village of Ben Suc as they progressed across the area. Ben Suc was a village with the reputation of being a central hub for the guerilla fighters. Working with South Vietnamese fighters, the US took the village, finding an extensive network of tunnels, which they subsequently destroyed. The civilians living in the village, many of them children, were relocated to a refugee camp that put them out of harm's way during the operation.

The Allied forces working as the 'hammer' part of the operation continued to sweep through the region, encountering some VC troops along the way. With few adequate defensive positions, the VC knew they had little chance of fighting against the western forces, so they fled.

Operation CEDAR FALLS began on January 8 and ended on January 26, 1967.[3] The western forces and South Vietnamese successfully cleared the vegetation and destroyed the tunnels used by the VC to transit the region.

The VC were also developing their tactics to better fight what they knew was a significantly superior force. The VC refused to engage with western forces in large numbers and for the most part, it meant there were never any real gains by American and South Vietnamese forces. The guerilla fighters had intimate knowledge of the local terrain and knew how to covertly transit in and out of the area. It took a while for western forces to realize the VC had the tactical upper hand; they were wearing the US troop and their allies down over time with only a few gains to show for their effort.

ENTERING WAR ZONE C

War Zone C was a part of III Corps and it was near War Zone D. Planners drew this zone on the border between South Vietnam and Cambodia, making it a fairly large VC hot spot. Since Cambodia sought to remain neutral, they carried out checks on the VC who passed through the borders into their country. American soldiers, however, were not permitted to enter Cambodia, as Cambodia was not an official participant in the war. This prohibition remained in place until President Richard Nixon allowed ground troops to enter the country in 1970. During the first five years of the war, the VC continued to flee from South Vietnam and into Cambodia.[4]

War Zone C was situated to the northwest of War Zone D, along the Cambodian border. The northern and western parts of the zone were bounded by the Cambodian border, and Highway 13 was a few miles to the east of the zone's eastern boundary; it included parts of the Binh Duong, Binh Long, and Tay Ninh provinces. Like the other locations where the western forces had fought, navigating through War Zone C was hindered by the environmental factors. In addition to a thick jungle devoid of obvious paths through most of it, parts of the zone were mountainous. This made it more difficult to dominate the ground, as western forces lacked local knowledge of the terrain, caves, and other potentially beneficial terrain factors, whereas the VC had intimate geographical knowledge of all the escape routes and hiding places. The region also harbored swamps that made it hard to traverse certain areas in a way similar to the problems western forces had encountered in the Plain of Reeds. These differing conditions all proved to hamper movements, especially given the need for troops' acclimatization prior to field maneuvers. When entering War Zone C, the intention was to engage with the enemy and quickly overwhelm them with superior tactics and firepower. This tactic often failed because commanders failed to appreciate the difficulties of operating in such densely vegetated and mountainous terrain.

Besides its proximity to a country that was not stopping the VC from repeatedly crossing the border, this zone was critical for the VC to plan and execute attacks in other locations farther away from the border. At the center of this zone was an abandoned town called Katum. Both the PAVN and the VC used this location for their operations since it was easy to escape to the north and across the border. Rumors circulated that the communist Vietnamese fighters had been using it as their headquarters. If the Allied western forces could dominate War Zone C, they hoped it would at least temporarily stop political activities from a perceived leadership hot spot in South Vietnam. Although the Allied western forces had assimilated new lessons from their success in War Zone D, new challenges awaited them in their next sphere of operations.

OPERATION JUNCTION CITY

Having successfully used the "hammer-and-anvil" strategy in January, the western forces adapted it for an even bigger operation named Operation JUNCTION CITY. The operation's commanding officer was Major General William E. DePuy, and he chose the name after his hometown in Kansas.[5] Having executed the quick sweeping strategy in January, he and the other military leaders incorporated the unique specialty of the Sky Soldiers; this time, the plan included an airborne assault conducted by the 173rd Airborne Brigade.

PLANNING OPERATION JUNCTION CITY

There were two primary objectives of this operation. The first was to act as a quick and efficient search-and-destroy mission to remove the 9th VC Division established in the area. Leaders called for the rapid deployment of paratroopers to surprise the enemy and catch them unaware, thus limiting their ability to escape. As a result, the Allied forces hoped to remove the guerilla fighters from the area entirely. This would cut off many of their supply chains so they could not get farther inland, including blocking the Ho Chi Minh Trail.

There was also word that the enemy Central Office of South Vietnam, known as the COSVN, had used this region to meet and strategize. Allied forces believed that the COSVN had a main line back to Hanoi. They strategized and worked with Hanoi to establish combat plans and psychological operations and find a path forward as the western forces shifted their focus to different regions. According to intelligence that the western units had collected, the military leaders believed that the COSVN was a more centralized and organized group that had headquarters somewhere to the southwest of Saigon. They jokingly referred to this imagined major military facility as a "Bamboo Pentagon."[6] This shows just how valuable a target the US command considered the facility. They considered it a planning center that was equivalent in value to the VC as the American Pentagon was to the US forces. This nickname also illustrates that the western militaries were associating the facility with the static and bureaucratic western version of a command center, one supported by vast staffs and replete with military leaders, none of which turned out to be the case.

The COSVN was not nearly so bureaucratic or static. It had formed long before the French had left the region. The North Vietnamese could not afford to have such an obvious target that would compromise their entire operation, especially since they were continually being attacked by nations with superior firepower. The COSVN was effectively a loose group of people exhibiting great mobility, running information and plans to different areas from the commanders in Hanoi.[7] They constructed their own temporary huts where they could conduct their business. This mobility and versatility afforded the COSVN great flexibility that enabled them to uproot and escape quickly as Allied forces arrived. COSVN remained in War Zone C because of the ease with which they could escape into Cambodia, where the Sky Soldiers could not legally attack them. They had a tacit familiarity with the mostly pathless jungle terrain that allowed them to slip away under virtually any circumstance.

Although the ground differed significantly from the terrain of Operation CEDAR FALLS, the template that the January operation established could apply to War Zone C with some modifications. This time, the military strategists planned a large-scale mass tactical assault that required 250 helicopters to bring the 845 paratroopers into the battle as a part of the hammer that would sweep the VC toward the blocking forces that were already supposed to be in place.

The reason planners opted to deploy paratroopers into this strategy was that it allowed for the largest number of soldiers to be dropped into the smallest space, thus saturating and dominating the ground speedily. Once on the ground, and capitalizing on the element of surprise, paratroopers could begin their sweep, giving the guerilla forces far less time to flee. Up to this point, planners had not used paratroops as a part of major operations, so military leaders thought it highly unlikely that the VC would expect such a move. The sudden aerial deployment of so many troops into an area was intended to strike fear into the VC as they realized the Allied troops' reach could quickly extend across Vietnam, possibly out-maneuvering them.

However, one of the primary problems with this approach was that the paratroopers were being sent into an area where the VC had superior knowledge of the terrain. Not only were the Sky Soldiers unfamiliar with the region, but they were also going into the region under canvass, making them incredibly vulnerable to ground attacks as they descended. One paratrooper later said that one way they could deal with the anxiety of being so open and exposed was to use the mantra "big sky, little bullet," reminding themselves they would be much smaller targets to the enemy.[1] Since paratroops had not been deployed against the VC, and given how more Allied soldiers seemed to be killed by booby traps and mines, there was some relief amongst soldiers with this new approach. Any mental relief they could find was welcome as they would be jumping during in daylight, making it far easier for the VC to see the paratroopers as they entered the range of their weapons.

THE EXECUTION OF THE LARGEST AIRBORNE OPERATION

General William Westmoreland commanded Vietnam, and he earned his pivotal position as a reward for his long and distinguished military career. His early military experience saw him commanding forces in World War II, and he held a higher position during the Korean War. Westmorland was famous for being a charismatic and inspirational leader who learned the names and faces of the soldiers he commanded, giving him a much stronger connection with his troops. Despite this, his planned strategy for Operation JUNCTION CITY was high-risk and would likely result in increased casualties, particularly as some soldiers would be easy targets as they descended from the aircraft to their positions on the drop zone. While a large-scale, mass tactical assault was meant to shock and overwhelm the enemy, robust supply chains were essential for the mission's success, as troops could only deploy with limited combat supplies due to parachute weight limitations. Further supply of follow-on ammunition, water, and food from the air were needed to maintain the momentum, otherwise light-scaled troops could quickly deplete their supplies. To further complicate matters, they could not drop supplies into the same drop zone as the troops for fear of crushing them. This constraint could limit the success of the operation, as once the US forces were separated from their superior resources, they could not be as effective as the quicker VC who were more comfortable in the local surroundings.

The VC were under the command of North Vietnamese Senior General Nguyen Chi Thanh. He had grown up as a peasant under the French government, rising against them and becoming a revolutionary. The French arrested him for these activities, getting a name as someone who would fight for Vietnam. Once he was released, Thanh progressed to the position of Vietnam Communist Party Politburo in the early part of the 1950s. He joined the PAVN and reached the position of political czar, making him more of a political figure than a military one. While he held this position, the forces were under the control of General Vo Nguyen Giap. The two men did not agree on the right way to conduct the war. Having been successful with their guerilla tactics, Giap wanted to continue using them, but Thanh wanted to use the more traditional method of initiating a large unit attack against the westerners. Giap called Thanh's method suicidal because he was well aware they could not stand against the vastly superior US firepower. Though there were three nations contributing to the battle, the American forces were far more numerous, and they had one of the biggest militaries in the world. Though he was more of a political figure, the party leaders agreed with Thanh's approach to attacking in much larger forces. Thanh saw this as a chance to raise the morale of the VC troops, as well as thinking that the Americans would leave just like the French if they sustained high enough casualties.

The western forces divided nine battalions into three brigades, similar to the way they had divided troops for Operation MARAUDER. The brigades were to be sent out to create the 'anvil' part of the strategy, setting up their position in an east-to-west blocking maneuver along the northern boundary of what was Route 246. Two additional brigades were to establish blocking positions farther north. They scheduled some to be dropped by helicopter while others were due to move into position over land. They took up their positions along Routes 4 and 22, creating a block along the east and west. The 'hammer' part of the operation was to be enacted by an infantry brigade and a regiment of armored cavalry. As they moved to squeeze the VC between themselves and the blocking forces, they were to look for the headquarters that the western military believed was in the area. In total, the western forces sent twenty-two battalions into Operation JUNCTION CITY, consisting of around 30,000 allied troops.

The operation started around sunrise on February 22, 1967, when an airstrike of B-52 bombers began attacking the location where the VC were thought to be hiding. They cleared the area of vegetation to prepare for a brigade to be dropped in the area in stages. Once the airstrike ended, the US 1st Division began boarding seventy Army helicopters. Their destination was Katum, where they began an air assault at 0720 hours. Simultaneously, helicopters dropped the 196th Light Infantry Brigade to where Routes 22 and 246 met. More troops were being trucked in along the routes.

At 0900 hours, Task Force 2-503, Sky Soldier paratroopers, were beginning the only parachute insertion of the war. As C-130 Hercules and C-123 Provider aircraft flew over the area, 845 soldiers descended, drawing some enemy fire as they neared the ground. Helicopter gunships quickly drove away many of the VC so that the paratroops could land safely and get into formation prior to proceeding to their objectives. The gunships were very successful in their efforts to protect the paratroopers, with only one soldier being wounded by enemy fire on the way to the ground. At 0915 hours, the first shipment of cargo parachutes was dispatched from C-130s, providing artillery, ammunition, and trucks for the troops on the ground. It took the troops roughly an hour to organize and prepare to move. They soon began moving rapidly north toward the blocking forces, creating a horseshoe to create a large net that would be hard for the VC to break.

Operation JUNCTION CITY had a nearly flawless start, creating an initial impression that it was going to be incredibly successful. It was also the largest single-day helicopter operation in the history of Army Aviation – a total of 249 helicopters had been used.[8] This expectation quickly faded as the troops progressed over the next five days. They covered a lot of ground without encountering the kinds of supply caches they had located in the earlier operations, and they certainly found nothing like a large headquarters with VC documents and plans. They found many small caches, including a COSVN Psychosocial Operations photo lab containing 120 reels of motion picture films, but they had been hoping for something much larger and more vital to the communists. In that period, a reported twenty-eight Americans and fifty-four VC were killed. Allied forces were not capturing or cornering nearly as many VC as they had hoped. Several decades later, in a book published by Dinh Thi Van, it was alleged that a VC spy in Saigon had learned of the operation ahead of time, giving the communists plenty of time to get out of the area before the operation started.[9] [10] Not all the VC left the area, but there weren't nearly as many VC in the area as the western forces expected.

The first significant firefight occurred on February 28, 1967, as the western forces found a larger group of VC soldiers roughly seven miles outside of Katum. These were the forces that Thanh wanted to send to face the Americans head-on. Ambushing the Americans, the VC sustained a nearly four-hour attack, killing twenty-five Americans. However, it also proved General Giap correct regarding how much better prepared the Americans were because the VC lost 167 soldiers. A similar fight occurred on March 3, and the fighting continued to pick up over the next few weeks.

By the beginning of April 1967, the VC had sustained far more losses than the western forces, demonstrating the significant risks of Thanh's approach. The VC had stopped trying to confront the American forces, as this kind of tactic inevitably cost the VC far more men than the western forces. They stopped most of the direct confrontations, including giving up the defense of their bases when large forces arrived. Instead of directly facing their enemies, the VC resorted to their earlier tactic of sniping when they could and leaving mines and booby traps to take care of the invading western soldiers.

With the VC no longer standing and fighting as they had in the beginning, the Sky Soldiers spent an increasing amount of time trying to trek through the thick jungle and looking out for booby traps. Eventually, the VC would cross over the Cambodian border, reestablishing the stalemate.

Realizing there was no justification to keep going after eighty-two days, Operation JUNCTION CITY ended on May 14th, 1967. Most of the western forces were removed from War Zone C, leaving only a small band of five Special Forces groups at strategic bases to monitor them for the possible return of the VC.

THE END OF THE OPERATION

Today, the success of Operation JUNCTION CITY is still debated, as only one of the main objectives was met (the establishment of Special Forces camps in the area). While some of the smaller objectives were achieved, the primary mission to find and destroy major command centers was unsuccessful, coupled with a much higher number of Allied casualties than expected. The operation did not find any major facilities or document caches. Since it was the largest operation of the war up to that point, there were also far greater western casualties than in previous missions:

> "The Vietnamese Ministry of Defense places the death toll at 2,728 KIA, thirty-four VC soldiers captured, and 139 soldiers deserting their position of duty. The US suffered 300 soldiers KIA and another 1,500 wounded, making Operation Junction City one of the major combat losses of the war."[11]

The enemy also suffered desertions, as some VC no longer wanted to fight when confronted with such a large, better-armed, and better-trained force.

Although the American fighters had found nothing remotely resembling the VC headquarters or facility, they acquired a lot of new weaponry, especially when the VC stopped trying to fight them directly. They captured roughly 600 tons of weapons, with many of them being small arms, as well as 810 tons of rice, which could feed the western troops. They found roughly 500 pages of reports, a paltry number compared to the large caches found during the early operations. However, it was still critical to see how the VC's plans and strategies had changed since Operation CRIMP.

Both sides learned lessons following the end of the operation, with the VC deciding that guerilla warfare was a better tactic, given their situation. As a celebrated Vietnamese fighter, General Giap showed he had chosen a method of fighting that minimized the VC losses while still hitting back at the American forces. The US saw the success of the paratroopers but continued to use helicopters to bring forces onto the battlefield instead of air-dropping troops into an area to begin an attack. Drop zones required large, flat areas devoid of rocks, tree stumps and other such obstacles that could present significant injury risk to paratroopers as they landed. They used armored units in overgrown areas to remove the foliage, which simplified the troop movements.

Following the operation, South Vietnam was in a much better position militarily. Their forces joined the western forces in Operation JUNCTION CITY, where they learned limited tactics that the US military used during the fighting, better VC detection methods. For a short period, the southern government had far fewer issues, as much of the VC had fled back into Cambodia. As there was a swelling occupation of Northern Vietnamese forces in Cambodia, it started to affect Cambodia negatively. It was becoming less of a strategic place for the VC and more of a base for a foreign power within Cambodia's borders.

THE PARACHUTE AND DAGGER: THE ORIGINS OF THE UNIT'S INSIGNIA

Following Operation JUNCTION CITY, the Sky Soldiers created their own unique insignia. They earned the nickname Sky Soldiers by proving it to be an accurate description of their capabilities, but the 173rd wanted a special way of identifying their own. An insignia was an effective way of recognizing others in their unit quickly. The unit had an insignia designed to do just that.

The design was based on their pivotal role in Operation JUNCTION CITY. The most easily identifiable element of the symbol is the parachute, and under it is the name "Sky Soldiers." Inside the parachute is an unsheathed sword pointing down, showing how they began their assaults. They would jump from planes, making the initial direction of their attack from the sky striking downward. It specifically refers to the jump at the beginning of Operation JUNCTION CITY in February 1967. On either side of the sword are lightning bolts, showing the Sky Soldiers' ability to move quickly and strike effectively when deployed.

The insignia also cleverly codes the brigade's designation into the icon "173rd." The sword represents the "1." There are "7" objects around it (two lightning bolts, two wings, and three parachute canopies). The canopies act as the number "3." This insignia is still used to represent the 173rd Airborne Brigade today.[12]

AFTER OPERATION JUNCTION CITY

Operation JUNCTION CITY was a turning point in the war. It led to a renewed commitment to troop increases and paved the way for bigger and more expansive operations to come, like Operation GREELEY, Operation FRANCIS MARION, and Operation SAM HOUSTON. Over the next year, the Pentagon focused its attention on Dak To, the capital of the Dak To District in the Kontum Province. The series of operations and engagements would have a bloody and significant impact.

THE BATTLE OF DAK TO – PART 1

The war continued to escalate throughout 1967, with one of the fiercest periods of the fighting occurring later in the year. After War Zone C had been considered more secure, the US began focusing its attention on Dak To and the surrounding regions. Although the US initially hesitated about escalating the war, it became fully committed following Operation JUNCTION CITY. The US continued to increase the number of soldiers involved in operations. This approach appeared antithetical to the goal of teaching the South Vietnamese to fight for themselves, and once again, the American people questioned the American government's intention in the region. The casualties continued to increase, and Americans at home were forced to face the realities of the conflict. "By November 1967, the number of American troops in Vietnam was approaching 500,000, and US casualties had reached 15,058 killed and 109,527 wounded."[1]

American troops continued to fight heavily in operations, and the US government touted the idea back home that they were winning the war in Vietnam. Meanwhile, the soldiers involved were developing skepticism about their actual success.

Early in the war, Lyndon Johnson assured the American public that the Vietnam conflict would be a short-term engagement. He claimed that by escalating the conflict, the US would effectively end it. He convinced the American public that overwhelming the enemy would inevitably lead to victory in the region and the South Vietnamese government achieving control of the entire country.

"Johnson sold this deployment to the US public by claiming that they would be in South Vietnam as a short-term measure. In a poll held in 1965, 80% of those Americans polled indicated that they supported Johnson."[2]

By 1967, the short, quick victory that most of the American people expected clearly was not going to happen, and the deployed soldiers realized how far the war was from ending. The Sky Soldiers had been in the country for two years by this time, and the fighting had been steadily escalating, which was obvious by the increased number of soldiers being sent into Vietnam. The draft did not begin in the US until December 1969, but the growing American presence was a sign of problems with the war, not a sign of winning.

The fighting in and around Dak To proved to be a brutal and grueling experience for many of the American soldiers deployed in the region. As the clashes between the western forces and VC became more intense, even the most hardened soldiers found the situation to be challenging on a new level.

ESTABLISHED PRESENCE IN THE REGION

While there was constant fighting and enemy movement around Vietnam since American soldiers had arrived, commanders deployed various units to key regions to ensure the VC did not return and undermine the South Vietnamese government. Typically, special forces were used to establish a discreet presence that was less obvious than a large unit. The US Special Forces Civilian Irregular Defense Group, known by the acronym CIDG, was a CIA program to recruit indigenous ethnic minorities in the region to the South Vietnamese cause. It was an effort to undermine VC recruitment in the area. According to Jeffrey J. Clarke's book *United States Army in Vietnam Advice and Support: The Final Years, 1965–1973*:

"The South Vietnamese National Police and the Civilian Irregular Defense Group (CIDG) were paramilitary organizations entirely separate from the armed forces. The CIDG consisted of company-size rifle units, organized and led by American and South Vietnamese Special Forces teams, but supported financially and logistically by the United States alone. Its members were recruited from South Vietnamese religious and ethnic minority groups living in remote areas inaccessible to the South Vietnamese government. Hired and paid by US Army Special Forces

'advisors,' the CIDG troops swore allegiance 'to no flag, no government.' ... In mid-1965 the CIDG program had between twenty thousand and twenty-five thousand members and the National Police between forty thousand and forty-five thousand men."[3]

The CIDG was initially issued orders to establish camps in the Kontum Province located close to the border with both Laos and Cambodia. The region fell into the II Corps strategic region, placing it northeast of the location where the Sky Soldiers spent the first couple of years of their deployment. The CIDG handled two major activities in this critical location. The first was to provide surveillance in the area to ensure that the PAVN and VC could not infiltrate the area. They also dedicated much of their time to training the people in the area, especially the villagers, who had little to no military experience with modern weaponry.

The CIDG established camps across the province, including near a critical village called Dak To. This village was vital because it had an airstrip. Once the camp was established, the village became a critical operations base for reconnaissance units that monitored the Ho Chi Minh Trail and North Vietnamese activity. The trail ran through the kingdoms of Cambodia and Laos, giving the PAVN and VC a more reliable path to supply and reinforce their troops, as well as move troops around after they fled instead of facing the western forces head-on.[4]

The US camp and the village of Dak To became a hot spot in 1967 as the VC, led by General Giap, continued to start skirmishes and small battles over several months. They drew out the Americans with these minor attacks, hoping to entice them into attacking them. Since they had the high ground and were entrenched in the locations where they attacked the US troops, they were able to gain an advantage.

This led to a series of skirmishes known colloquially as the hill fights. Giap had his men lure American soldiers to these locations to devastating effects, demoralizing American troops in Vietnam.

A NERVE CENTER FOR THE VC

The number of skirmishes started by the VC and other communist forces was increasing, especially in the Dak To region, which became one of a few flash points for the war. Enemy forces considered the region a part of the South Vietnamese highlands, creating a precarious region for soldiers unfamiliar with it. Besides the hills and easy places to hide for those who knew the area, part of what made the region particularly dangerous was that it was near two borders with two countries that the VC used to infiltrate and then escape from South Vietnam. By 1967, the communists had established Base Area 609, one of the primary locations for strategizing, sending supplies, and managing their troops. It was one of the nerve centers near the Ho Chi Minh Trail, ensuring they could communicate easily and send word to other leaders.[4]

Since the region was heavily foliaged, few civilians lived in the area. US Forces established the barracks in 1965 and the fighting that followed from 1966 until 1972 has often been said to have been some of the fiercest. By the summer of 1967, the VC and PAVN were initiating battles in the Kontum Province. They began launching mortars at the US camp, drawing the attention of the military strategists. The commander of the special forces was Colonel Jonathan Ladd and once he learned the camp was being attacked, the commander headed to the Dak To camp. He quickly organized troops and sent them on a reconnaissance mission to locate where the attacks were originating. The soldiers found a small bunker complex positioned in a way that allowed it to be attacked easily, but taking it out would be far more difficult if it had not been abandoned. Ladd notified his superiors of the findings, with Major General William Peers being the man who would get to decide how they would handle it. Peers' response was to use a heliborne assault on the bunker, which immediately upset Ladd. Having learned about Peers' decided course of action, Ladd reportedly replied, "For God's sake, General, don't send our people in there. That's what the bastards want us to do. They'll butcher our people. If they want to fight us, let them come down here where we can kill them."[5]

Peers did not listen, having determined that a search-and-destroy operation was the best path forward, sadly a tactic that General Giap successfully exploited. Giap knew the Americans thought they were superior in terms of firepower and war-fighting capabilities but anticipated they would underestimate the recognized Vietnamese general and his strategic skills.

For most of 1967, Dak To appeared the most likely location for an inevitable face-off with enemy forces. Starting in April, both sides tried to weaken or remove the other. By November, Dak To was about to earn the reputation that it continued to have over the course of the war. It was one of the few locations where the VC initiated and sustained fighting against the Americans with devastating effects on both sides.

OPERATIONS SAM HOUSTON AND FRANCIS MARION

There had been intermittent fighting in and around Dak To in early 1967, which began to ramp up as US forces initiated planned operations. The US conducted Operation SAM HOUSTON between February 12 and April 5 deploying the 2nd Brigade, 4th Infantry Division, into the Plei Trap Valley to establish a base in the region. After landing, C Company, 1st Battalion, found a series of abandoned bunkers near the landing zone (LZ).[6] Within the first twenty-four hours of their arrival, PAVN ambushed C Company, though the ambush was pushed back quickly. Commanders sent more American troops into the region, and ambushes continued to occur often. Within a day, they lost fifty-five soldiers, and seventy-four more sustained injuries.[6] The PAVN lost nearly 300, but the prevalence and ferocity of the ambushes alarmed General Peers, who was not nearly so willing to risk his own men just for clearing patrols. For five days, they kept these patrols closer to the LZ. To remove as many PAVN as possible, they conducted mortar attacks and air strikes in the regions beyond the patrols. When reinforcements arrived, patrols began moving farther from the LZ.

While some American strategists considered the area now

clear of PAVN, there was ample evidence this was not the case. Commanders ordered American soldiers to withdraw and take up a position in Plei Doc, however this allowed the PAVN and VC to continue infiltrating the region as the US did not maintain a large presence near the border. During this time, the PAVN started "hugging" the American units, meaning they were too close to the Americans for air strikes and artillery to be effective, leaving American forces struggling to counter this tactic. US forces eventually found the M79 40mm grenade launchers were among the best weapons to use in a jungle setting whilst PAVN units were close to them. Because of its distinctive firing sound, the launcher earned the name "thumper" or "thump-gun" with the troops and was used with good effect in the close-quarter battles of the jungle where effective artillery support was often lacking.[6]

Ultimately, Operation SAM HOUSTON was not as successful as US military decision-makers had hoped it would be. While the enemy took a significant number of casualties, the PAVN was able to dictate the timing and location of the engagements leading to the US forces taking more casualties than they expected. American military strategists had been planning Operation FRANCIS MARION over much of the early part of 1967, using some of what had been learned from Operation SAM HOUSTON and the PAUL REVERE series of operations, the latter being conducted near the same area and following many of the same strategies as Operation SAM HOUSTON.[6] The FRANCIS MARION operation determined how to best approach securing the area around the camps at Plei Djereng, Plei Me, and Duc Co. US commanders tasked several special forces units with conducting longer-range reconnaissance missions to the west of the area, bringing them closer to the Cambodian border. The Americans used the CIDG units and the 4th Infantry Division to conduct these operations, while the ARVN supplemented the forces along the southern area. The ARVN acted as an initial screen in the Darlac Province while another unit, the 42nd Regiment of the ARVN, extended the screen up into the Kontum Province, providing some connection with the city of Kontum and the established camp at Tan Canh Base.

During the initial, lengthy battles of Operation FRANCIS MARION, it became clear the successful tactics employed by the PAVN during Operation SAM HOUSTON had become a template for the those subsequently used against the Americans in FRANCIS MARION. As a result, American troops also adopted the counter-tactics that helped them, including the use of the M576 40mm grenades in the jungles; yet, just like in previous operations, when the fighting became too intense, the PAVN and VC simply moved over the Cambodian border where the US and South Vietnamese forces could not follow them.

The US adopted a slightly different method of attack that was literally hit-or-miss; for example, commanders sent an air strike into the Ia Drang Valley on July 10, with the attacks taking place roughly 5 km from the Cambodian border. American commanders sent the 1/12th Infantry to follow into the area on the ground on July 11 to assess the damage from the strike and found no initial evidence the PAVN had been in the area. The next day however, C Company of the 1/12th encountered a large PAVN force nearby and called in another air strike and artillery to deal with the enemy forces. C Company were soon pinned down, and when B Company was sent in to reinforce them, they also became encircled. By this point, the fog had rolled in, making air support unsafe. Artillery was used to prevent the PAVN from overrunning the companies, but one round mistakenly struck the command group of B Company, killing several Americans, including the commander. It wasn't until after the fog cleared that air strikes were possible to eventually drive back the PAVN forces. Most of the casualties occurred in B Company, with thirty-one dead, seven missing, and six being taken as POWs. The POWs remained prisoners until 1973.[6]

Following an ambush on August 3 near the Dak Seang Camp, the American troops took another prisoner. They interrogated him for more information, and he said the PAVN was planning to attack Dak Pek Camp and Dak Seang Camp. The American military strategists responded to this report by sending ARVN forces and the 1st Airborne Task Force to the region to patrol Dak Seang. This time, they encountered a large force, resulting in a four-day battle, ending with the ARVN successfully driving the PAVN out of the area and north into Laos. After the PAVN left, the AVRN found more plans that included an attack on Dak Seang Camp that was planned for August 6.

When the operation ended on October 11, the military strategists declared it a success. General Westmoreland proudly announced, "I am absolutely certain that whereas in 1965 the enemy was winning, today he is certainly losing!"[7] Other military leaders and major American politicians seized this idea, giving Americans a false sense that the war, which was now several years old, was going well. They made it sound like the tides had turned, even giving the impression that the war would not last much longer. This was far from the truth, as the next few operations made clear.

OPERATION GREELEY

As the fighting during Operation FRANCIS MARION continued to escalate over the summer of 1967, American military strategists were already planning Operation GREELEY. This was essentially a troop reinforcement combined with another search-and-destroy operation that wedded the joint efforts between the US 4th Infantry Division, the Sky Soldiers, and the ARVN, starting June 17, 1967. The focus was on Dak To because there was a growing PAVN and VC presence in the area.

The first major engagement of this operation occurred roughly seven and a half miles south of the Ben Het and nearly nine miles from the Cambodian border at a hill called Hill 830, indicating the number of meters above sea level (approximately 2,724 feet).[8] This location was one of the major points along the Ho Chi Minh Trail and was a valuable location the US wanted to secure.

Sky Soldiers from the 4th Battalion, 503rd Infantry, were ordered to attack a large PAVN force in the region on July 10, 1967, and B Company was to lead in follow on forces to support shortly afterwards. B Company's orders were changed at short notice and subsequently sent to a different location. Each of the companies headed in separate directions to achieve their search-and-destroy objectives.

Activities began around 1545 hours, with A Company quickly encountering some enemy fire. After assessing the situation, the American troops determined there was a small, entrenched group of PAVN with two bunkers housing light machine guns. A Company quickly requested artillery support to deal with this small force that had pinned down one platoon. One of the other platoons maneuvered around the enemy and artillery fire to assist the soldiers trapped in their current location. The rescuing platoon had to work off the last communication from the trapped platoon, as their commanding officer had gone radio silent, and it was evening before contact with the pinned-down platoon was reestablished. By this time, the artillery strikes had successfully taken out the two light machine guns, but all three of the platoons were engaged in heavy fire against the PAVN forces.

D Company had been following A Company, but when they learned that A Company was under mortar fire, they shifted their movements to provide support. As they repositioned themselves, D Company came under heavy fire from their right flank. Since B Company was located farther to D Company's right, they adjusted their position to attack the PAVN from the northeast. However, they also quickly came under heavy fire from mortars and more undiscovered bunkers housing light machine guns, killing and injuring many B Company forces, including the company commander.

D Company moved to reinforce B Company, sending two platoons to their last known location, and a third platoon to assist A Company, who had lost contact when they tried to move closer to B Company. At 1800 hours, the two D Company platoons heading to reinforce B Company reached them and they prepared to bunker down for the night. After battling some light fire and the terrain, the third D Company platoon attempted to radio A Company to let them know they could not reach them until after nightfall. Some attempts were made to take the wounded and dead out of the area, but the weather and repeated attacks made extraction difficult. As a result, only three injured soldiers were evacuated from the area during the night.

Between July 11 and July 12, the American forces were able to reorganize themselves, reconsolidate, and establish a presence around the area they had been sent to secure. Evacuation of the injured and killed was eventually achieved, leaving the rest of the forces to conduct another search-and-destroy mission in the vicinity. US forces primarily moved in daylight hours and found more tunnels and trenches that were being used by the PAVN and VC for quick withdrawals. Three different, robust base camps were discovered by the end of July 12.

Operation GREELEY was one of the first instances in which American casualties were far greater than those of the communists. The PAVN and VC lost nine soldiers, and a tenth was taken prisoner. The US lost twenty-five soldiers, and a further sixty-two sustained injuries that required them to be evacuated from the area for treatment. One soldier, Specialist Peter Lechnir, who suffered a significant injury on Hill 830, later died in 1973 because of his injuries. All this occurred during a single day, July 10. Command issued their official quarterly report on July 31, 1967, detailing many of the events that showed what went wrong on the first day of the operation. This was only the beginning of a costly fight that saw the loss of many lives, with Americans, PAVN, VC, and ARVN all suffering substantially.

6

THE BATTLE OF DAK TO – PART 2
HILL 875

Operation GREELEY, the effort to sweep the jungle-covered mountains of the Kontum province, culminated in the Battle of Hill 875. Like Hill 830, Hill 875 was named because of its height in meters above sea level, which roughly equates to half a mile. Looking up the hill from the bottom, US soldiers knew they faced a brutal and dangerous fight if they wanted to make it to the top and secure it.

At 0943 hours, November 19, 1967, the Battle of Hill 875 began. US soldiers, including several companies of the 173rd, began making their way up the hill searching for embedded VC and North Vietnamese soldiers. US forces found they were walking into a series of ambushes that proved to be very costly and sadly, many Sky Soldiers lost their lives in the chaos. One such Sky Soldier was Private First Class Carlos Lozada of the 2nd Battalion, 503 Infantry, 173rd Airborne Brigade. When Private Lozado's company was ambushed, he bravely covered the retreat of his fellow soldiers before falling. Lozado was posthumously awarded the Medal of Honor. The citation stated:

"Private First Class Lozada apparently realized that if he abandoned his position, there would be nothing to hold back the surging North Vietnamese soldiers and that the entire company withdrawal would be jeopardized. He called for his comrades to move back and that he would stay and provide cover for them. He made this decision, realizing that the enemy was converging on three sides of his position and only meters away, and a delay in withdrawal meant almost certain death. Private First Class Lozada continued to deliver a heavy, accurate volume of suppressive fire against the enemy until he was mortally wounded and had to be carried during the withdrawal. His heroic deed served as an example and an inspiration to his comrades throughout the ensuing four-day battle."[1]

In response to the many PAVN and VC ambushes, US forces broke into smaller groups to locate enemy enclaves, at which point they could call in air support and use its superior technology to give the Sky Soldiers on the ground an advantage.

"In addition to the US Marine A-4 [aircraft], a pair of US Air Force A-1 Skyraiders was dropping napalm—intending both to kill North Vietnamese troops and to create fires on the ground that the pilots in faster A-4s could use as reference points for follow-on bombing runs."[2]

Over the course of the day, Captain Dick Goetze, an Air Force pilot, flew over the command center to assess the situation in his AC-130 Spectre Gunship. He was eventually ordered to depart the area so B-52 strategic bombers could carpet-bomb the vicinity later that day. Having seen the situation on the ground, Goetze disobeyed the orders, saying, "They'd [the bombs] just wipe everybody out."[5] Despite his warnings, the decision was made to proceed with bombing efforts. At 1858hrs, two A-4 Skyhawk fighter-bombers were sent out to execute the order to bomb the VC and PAVN forces in the area.

Unfortunately for US troops on the ground, Goetz was right. In the confusion, two 500-pound bombs were dropped on US soldiers, killing over 20 US troops. According to the investigation into the incident, Lieutenant Colonel Richard Taber, US Marines, was the pilot flying over to drop the bomb on the VC nearby. Taber's expertise was relied upon, since he had experience with similar missions, having flown ninety combat hours in three months. Taber and his wingman's mission was to drop "Snakeye" MK-81 "dumb" bombs (fitted with fins to slow the bombs' descent and allow the aircraft time to clear the blast radius) on one of the surrounding napalm fires, but the bombs fell roughly 650 feet short of the destination, directly hitting trees and exploding overhead C Company's command center. One of the bombs failed to detonate otherwise the casualty count could have been higher. This demonstrated how Goetze had made the right call; the bombings were simply too close to the soldiers on the ground. Friendly fire struck the US command post and medical area, killing many US soldiers. The investigation into the events of November 19, 1967 has raised questions that are still debated to this day.

Regardless of what happened, the human cost of the mistake is undeniable. Specialist Jon Cook was among those in the area, working as one of the few radio operators who had survived the rough, week-long fighting. He had originated in another company but become separated in the fighting, so had joined C Company's command post.

Specialist Cook was near a pile of tree trunks that had broken over the course of the fighting when a bomb struck the impromptu command center and the ground shook nearby. Initially, he thought the VC and PAVN were moving forward and had successfully struck against them. Then he heard another operator shout into the radio, "Stop! You're killing us!" That was when he realized it was "blue-on-blue," nomenclature for an errant attack on friendly forces by the Marine Corp's A-4 Skyhawk pilots.[2]

Though the fighting was intense and brutal, it allowed the opportunity for heroism, and many members of the 173rd stepped up to display their courage and compassion on the battlefield. One such courageous Sky Soldier was the battalion's chaplain, Major Charles Watters, who boosted morale by saying mass, by providing comfort to the wounded, and by delivering last rites to the dying. During some of the fighting, he actually slipped out to rescue wounded soldiers who could not get back on their own. Depending on their injuries, he helped them stumble back, carried them, or dragged them back to the hill for treatment. Though he was not required to be so close to combat, he selflessly did what he could to help the soldiers without killing anyone himself. By this point, there were a few remaining radio operators, and the medics were working frantically to help the wounded who could return to the camp. Chaplain Watters saw an opportunity to aid the wounded and took it upon himself to do so. Ultimately, he lost his life in the process.[3]

As one of the other survivors, Warrant Officer Stephen Green, later said of the report about the event, "The report could not show the desperation and extreme courage displayed in abundance. And it certainly did not explain what each of the survivors must live with forever."[4] Cook was one of those survivors. He moved over the lip of the crater, crawling over it as the smoke was still coming out of the center. One of the first things he noticed was the body parts lying around on the ground. Then he heard the moaning and crying coming out of the smoking crater. This was when he realized the command post had taken a hit, so he moved forward, trying to assist where he could. One of his friends called to him, but it became clear once Cook reached him that the friend was going to bleed to death. There was nothing Cook could do as the soldier tragically lost both legs from the middle of his thighs. Cook then found a medic with a shattered arm. He continued to move around the crater, doing what he could for the soldiers who were still alive. Since they did not yet know they had been victims of friendly fire, the survivors prepared for an attack, believing they were likely to be attacked and finished off soon. It was only after no one came that the realization sank in that it had not been the North Vietnamese who caused the destruction.

The total casualty count is disputed, (some of the missing were never found) though it is thought to be between twenty and forty-five Americans killed, including the Chaplin, who was awarded the Medal of Honor posthumously for risking himself to rescue soldiers. Another ten soldiers were wounded in the friendly fire. Three soldiers were never found. Following the tragic strike, most of the remaining leaders in the area and the medics were dead or seriously injured.

The event at Hill 875 was one of the deadliest instances of friendly fire during the war, and blue-on-blue attacks remained a serious risk to American ground forces for decades. Lieutenant Colonel Taber, the A-4 Skyhawk pilot, was unrepentant in his mission report on the incident, blaming everyone else but himself, even championing his prior successful strike rate with the Snakeye bombs. Years later, he admitted his superior had grounded him for three days after the incident but then ordered him back into the cockpit, which he saw as absolution by commanders. During the 1990s, fratricide incidents were reduced with the introduction of smart weapons and advanced targeting technologies, but for American forces in the Vietnam War, fighting in the thick jungles with poor visibility, chaotic ground troop movements, and enveloped in the true fog of war, it was sadly far harder for pilots to avoid such incidents.

In 2017, Cook joined others as they returned to the area to find the three soldiers who were never found. The three soldiers were Sergeant Donald Landoli, Specialist Jack Croxdale II, and Private First Class Benjamin David De Herrera. To this day, no remains of the soldiers have been located. Cook believes they were probably vaporized by the bomb. However, the trip seemed to help Cook, as he connected with others who had been there, along with one of the investigators who had written the report. Though he said that he has tried to move past the trauma of his experience, having become a father and a grandfather, he said that not a day has gone by when he hasn't thought about that day in history.[4]

OPERATION MACARTHUR

Despite the heavy losses of the Battle of Dak To, Operation GREELEY achieved several of its objectives and ceased in October 1967. It pushed PAVN and VC forces back from the Kontum province, sending them back over the border into Cambodia, and the Sky Soldiers also managed to obtain valuable intelligence. This success set the stage for Operation MACARTHUR in mid-October 1967.

The operation's major focus was securing the Central Highlands, with the primary force in the area being the 4th Infantry Division. Sky Soldiers involved in the operation were responsible for protecting both the urban and rural capitals located on or near Highway 14 from the PAVN and VC. Highway 14 was a paved road, which was a significant difference from many other operations that focused on regions that were far less developed.

The primary PAVN and VC headquarters along the highway were under the command of General Hoang Minh Thao. The reach of Thao's command went through several provinces in South Vietnam, including western Binh Dinh, Darlac, Kontum, western Phu Bon Province, and Pleiku Province, and Highway 14 was one of the primary nerve routes used by the communists as it had a direct connection to the Ho Chi Minh trail.

General William Rosson was the commander of the American forces during this time.

Toward the end of 1967, Rosson noticed a growing VC and PAVN presence along the highway and around the Central Highlands. Guessing this was a sign of an impending offensive, Rosson evaluated the region to determine what the enemy's most likely targets would be. Based on the troops, resources, and likely strategies, Rosson thought the offensive would mostly likely be against the camps controlled by the CIDG. The CIDG's camps were mainly in the western part of the Kontum Province and across the Pleiku Province, and both locations were close to the Cambodian border, where the PAVN and VC had a large base. Since Dak To was an important part of the region, it became part of the focus for both sides.

Acting on this belief, Operation MACARTHUR began on November 3. The early phase was fairly simple as Rosson moved troops around the areas where fighting was likely to occur. Phase one was wrapped up by November 24, 1967, and the Sky Soldiers did very little over December as strategists planned for phase two, which would begin in the early part of the following year.

ESCALATION AT THE BEGINNING OF 1968 – THE TET OFFENSIVE

Since the beginning of the operation, there had been little PAVN activity along Highway 14. This ended on January 15, 1968, when a forty-vehicle American convoy was moving along the highway just west of the village of An Khe, and three mines were detonated as the convoy passed by. The explosions were followed by small arms fire and rocket-propelled grenade attacks. Reacting quickly, the Sky Soldiers divided up and returned fire from different locations.

Specialist Dwight H. Johnson, was a tank driver from B

Company and was part of the force that reacted to the attack. Since he was further back in the convoy, away from the initial point of contact, he pressed forward until his tank became too damaged to go any further forward. Once he reached the point of the explosions, he did not want to remain in the vehicle. Johnson took his .45 caliber pistol to help the his fellow Sky Soldiers who had been caught in the initial attack. Thankfully he was a good shot, killing several of the PAVN soldiers before running out of ammunition. Without another weapon on him, Johnson returned to the tank, which was now drawing much heavier fire (including antitank weapons) to retrieve a submachine gun. Once in possession, he returned to the fighting, reaching the center of the ambush. When he once again ran out of ammunition, Johnson was caught in the center of the ambush with no other long-range weapon. Since he was already up close, Johnson flipped the gun and used the stock end to kill the closest PAVN. Again, without a weapon, he went to another nearby tank, where he found a wounded soldier. Prioritizing the soldier over weapons, Johnson carried his fallen fellow soldier and took him to a personnel carrier to be treated. With that task completed, he returned to the tank. At first, he used the main gun for as long as it worked, then once it jammed, he found a .45 caliber pistol. Fighting his way back to his original tank, Johnson reached it, where he started using the externally mounted machine gun. This meant he stayed out in the open, an easy target if there had been any snipers or sharpshooters available on the PAVN's side. He continued shooting at the enemy until reinforcements arrived to help secure the area. Johnson had entirely ignored his own personal safety, rescuing and saving many soldiers who could not fight back, and in so gallantly doing, was awarded the Medal of Honor.[5]

Fighting continued over much of January and February 1968 in and around Dak To, proving that Rosson's assessment had almost certainly been correct. Both months proved particularly bloody, with the US losing 463 men by the end of February. The PAVN and VC sustained much greater casualties—2,806 soldiers by the end of February.

This period was known as the Tet Offensive. The PAVN and VC planned a large offensive all across South Vietnam. They initiated ambushes of both civilian and military centers during a period of celebration for the Vietnamese. This meant that the civilian-run areas and places where the ARVN were in control had far fewer people in place because they were on leave. The hope was to incite more rebellions across South Vietnam and destabilize the government. Initially, they were successful because no one expected the fierce offensive attack, especially since that was not how the Northern Vietnamese had strategized up to that point in the war. Some cities were lost at the beginning of this phase, but the Americans and ARVN retook the cities and pushed the VC and PAVN out of most of the regions. When it ended, the US considered the Tet Offensive a significant defeat for the communists as it had not resulted in mass rebellions or South Vietnamese people defecting to their side.

One unexpected but significant effect it had, though, was to turn the opinion of the American public, who saw the initial losses as significant. Given the American's superior numbers and firepower, the fact that the Northern Vietnamese could enact such a large attack without being swiftly put down, was a significant blow to American morale. It further showed that the American military had seriously underestimated the abilities of the communists, or they had lied to the American people, neither of which was an acceptable scenario for American citizens. As General Westmoreland called for another 200,000 troops to be brought forward, even the most dedicated supporters of the war rethought their view, especially as it had already been almost a year since they had been told that the communists were losing. The Tet Offensive had proved this was far from the truth, making a large percentage of Americans strongly question both the military's ability to fight and the need for the US to be involved.

FOLLOWING THE TET OFFENSIVE

A new division commander, Major General Charles Stone, assumed command in March 1968. His plan focused on reconnaissance patrols around the Cambodian and Laotian borders. His soldiers were supported by helicopters and scouting planes. This meant that any PAVN they encountered were defeated easily. Stone was not interested in going too far from the established region because as he said, "I have everything the enemy wants, and he has nothing I want." Instead of letting his men be led into traps, as had been the case during 1967, he waited for the PAVN and VC to come to his troops, where they could then be significantly outmatched.

March began with troops spread out all along the Darlac, Kontum, and Pleiku Provinces, with an eye on Ban Me Thuot. For the first couple of days, the PAVN and VC withdrew to recuperate and reorganize after the failure of the Tet Offensive. General Thao changed his plans for the area, deciding to threaten the forces there more often and with little intent to control it. Since the American presence was so large in this region, he realized it would be more productive to attack in locations where there were fewer troops.

Perhaps disillusioned following the significant failure of the Tet Offensive, one of the PAVN commanders, Vu Nhu Y, turned himself over to the American troops on March 1, 1968. They took him in for interrogation, and he told them that General Thao planned to draw more American troops to the region to make it easier to attack other parts of South Vietnam. He also told the US that the North Vietnamese troops in the area were still recovering from the fierce fighting of the last few months, though reinforcements were on the way, and some had already arrived.

It did not take long before General Thao enacted some of his plan. March proved to be much less violent, with most of the fighting being short-lived. With an idea of what was coming, the US strategists brought all the Sky Soldiers into the Binh Dinh Province, where they were to trade places with the 3rd Brigade, 4th Infantry Division. For the first time since the war began, three major brigades were in the same area. The calm of March quickly gave way to more intensive fighting.

THE STEADY FIGHTING THROUGH JANUARY 1969

April saw the escalation of enemy attacks. For the first half of the month, the PAVN made some strategic ambushes, distracting from their real plan. On April 15, US troops located west of Firebase 14 came under heavy fire. As two communist deserters reported on April 20, the plan was to engage in more attacks to infiltrate the American forces. This area was important to the VC and PAVN because of its proximity to all three of the country's borders, as well as being close to major cities. In response to these reports, Stone established another outpost close to the firebase to counter increased forces.

April proved to be a far bloodier and more destructive month as both sides nearly doubled the number of casualties they sustained. This escalation continued over the rest of 1968 and into January 1969. Even if the VC and PAVN's original plan was to find areas with less American presence, this area with a large American force was still critical to the communists, so they could not entirely give up on trying to break down the American units to reestablish their supply lines and presence.

By the time it ended, Operation MACARTHUR had become one of the longest-running operations the Americans had initiated throughout the war; it also ended as one of the bloodiest.

The victory proclaimed in the early part of 1968 was clearly wrong, and Americans back home were losing patience and faith that the American military would be in any way successful.

THE OUTCOME OF THE BATTLE OF DAK TO

The Battle of Dak To was one of the most costly and bloody periods the Sky Soldiers experienced. From a strategic standpoint, it was successful because the Americans and ARVN retained control of an area that the PAVN and VC wanted to access more readily. The Battle of Dak To resulted in 376 American deaths, 79 ARVN deaths, and 1,441 Americans wounded. The estimated number of deaths of the PAVN was between 1,000 and 1,445. Despite American forces effectively driving back a large proportion of the PAVN division, the remaining PAVN forces were still able to accomplish one of their primary objectives; the PAVN drew Americans away from the more populated areas, leaving cities and towns vulnerable during the Tet Offensive.

Once the Tet Offensive ended, fighting in the region worsened. The PAVN and VC found it far harder to reestablish their presence since more American forces were now located in an important region for North Vietnamese reinforcements and supplies.

Ultimately, both sides made mistakes that later came back to cause them problems over the course of the war.

The Battle of Dak To remains a period of success for the US military, although the Sky Soldiers sacrificed much to lay the foundation for a successful outcome and ultimately, paid the highest price.

"The 173rd Airborne Brigade ... served in Vietnam for a total of 2,301 days and holds the record for the longest continuous service under fire of any American unit, ever. During that six-year, three-plus-month period, the 173rd lost 1,601 (roughly 31%) of its men—killed in action."[6]

The events that took place at Dak To were some of the most intense periods of fighting, during which the Sky Soldiers sustained the highest number of casualties.

One of the most emblematic examples of this sacrifice and heroism is the story of John Andrew Barnes III. On November 12, 1967, as the battle for Dak To was intensifying, North Vietnamese forces attacked Barnes' unit. The Vietnamese forces initially had the upper hand in the battle, killing a manned machine gunner. Barnes rushed to take control of the weapon, killing nine VC soldiers in retaliation. However, his heroism did not stop there. Shortly afterwards, a grenade landed among wounded American soldiers, and in an act of pure heroism, Barnes threw his body onto the grenade, sacrificing himself to save the lives of his fellow Sky Soldiers. Barnes was posthumously awarded the Medal of Honor for his bravery.[7]

The Battle of Dak To will forever stand out as a stark example of the bravery of the Sky Soldiers and the ultimate sacrifice made by American soldiers.

7

FAMOUS LEADERS OF THE 173RD

In a letter to the captains of the Virginia Regiment in July 1759, George Washington famously said, "Discipline is the soul of an army. It makes small numbers formidable; procures success to the weak and esteem to all."[1] The spirit of this notion is present in the leadership of the 173rd, over 200 years later.

The best military leaders are often forged by experiencing difficult and life-threatening situations, where one must learn to balance the safety of their soldiers with achieving the mission. True leaders must have the ability to inspire people to do things that are sometimes against human nature, and their courage and charisma are often instrumental in leading their soldiers into battle, having already experienced tragic and devastating events. With such a long career fighting in Vietnam, several distinguished military leaders emerged from the Sky Soldiers.

This chapter looks at three of the most influential leaders of the Sky Soldiers.

William Ray Peers, known to his inner circle as Ray, was born in 1914 in rural Stuart, Iowa. Following his graduation from high school, Peers was accepted into the University of California, which he attended in Los Angeles. He joined the Sigma Pi fraternity and graduated in 1937 with a degree in education. The following year, he received a commission in the US Army. Following Pearl Harbor and the declaration that the US was joining World War II, he was recruited into the Office of Strategic Services, where he joined Detachment 101 and was sent to fight in the Pacific Theater against the Japanese. During his time there, he was involved in guerilla tactics against the Japanese. He was eventually promoted to unit commander. In 1945, he was again promoted, this time to be the commander of operations in the southern part of the Yangtze River. Under this new role, he led Nationalist Chinese parachuters into Nanjing to finally remove the Japanese, who had committed countless atrocities in the city when they took it over in January 1938.

Following the end of the war, he became a CIA agent. In his new position, he created the first training program for the intelligence agency. He participated in the Korean War as an operative who helped mobilize Chinese Nationalist troops from Burma (Myanmar) and into the People's Republic of China.

Following the Korean War, Peers returned to the military, attending the Army War College. He held several positions. Since he had already fought in Asia, he was considered a good fit for a role in the Vietnam War. When the war began, he held the position of Assistant Deputy Chief of Staff of Special Operations. This job made sense, as he had been a part of several important operations in Asia. The next year, he was promoted to Special Assistant for Counterinsurgency and Special Activities for the Joint Chiefs of Staff. By January 1967, he was Major General Peers, and they appointed him the 32nd Commanding

Officer of the 4th Infantry Division. He continued to be promoted as the war progressed, and he was in charge of many of the most aggressive American formations in and around the Central Highlands. He also worked with the South Vietnamese and trained them for operations. He was instrumental in the Battle of Dak To and Duc Lap.

Peers utilized intelligence gleaned from a PAVN defector to engage with the enemy in favorable circumstances.[2] This utilization of intelligence led to many successes early in the battle of Dak To. Peers was also instrumental in defending Duc Lap Camp, which was attacked by PAVN forces from August 24 to August 27.[3] He orchestrated the defense of the camp, using various regiments as well as the South Vietnamese army, of whom he said "demonstrated professionalism and a fighting spirit equal to that of any unit in the history of the war."[4] His decision-making is credited with successfully defending the installation.

In 1969, General Westmoreland turned to him to investigate the actions at the My Lai Massacre, where between 347 and 504 unarmed people were killed by US army personnel. They chose Peers because he had a reputation for being fair and objective.[5] The subsequent 1970 report was called the *Peers Commission*. There were a few American soldiers who tried to stop the other American soldiers from committing the atrocities that were carried out. One of those few who tried to stop events was Hugh Thompson, who said of the report, "…He conducted a very thorough investigation. Congress did not like his investigation at all, because he pulled no punches, and he recommended court-martial for I think thirty-four people. Not necessarily for the murder, but for the cover-up."[6]

That was his final major contribution to the war. He went on to co-author several books between 1963 and 1979. Peers died of a heart attack on April 6, 1984, aged 70.

JOHN R. DEANE JR

Born John Russell Deane Jr. on June 9, 1919, he grew up with his family in San Francisco, California. With a father who was an Army Officer, it seemed like he would always follow in his father's footsteps. As soon as he was of age, Deane enlisted with the 16th Infantry. Then he joined the US Military Academy the next year. After graduating in 1942, he became the platoon leader of the 104th Infantry Division. He ended his time in World War II as a battalion commander.[7]

Between 1945 and 1954, they continually moved him back and forth between Europe and Washington, DC. This ended when he entered the Armed Forces Staff College, where he graduated. Deane then attended the National War College. By 1961, he had become the Commander of the 2nd Battle Group stationed in the West German part of Berlin. He was again promoted and returned to the US in 1962. By 1965, he had earned the position of Assistant Division Commander, 82nd Airborne Division, based at Fort Bragg, North Carolina.

In February of the next year, Deane finally received an assignment in Vietnam, where he served as the Chief of Staff for the Field Forces. His acts of heroism from November 5 through November 18, 1966, earned him one of his Distinguished Service Crosses. Upon learning of a group of American soldiers being overwhelmed by VC forces, he flew his helicopter into an insecure area, drawing enemy fire and firing upon the enemy. He then made his way to the front line to extract wounded soldiers. He did this all while wearing a cast on his leg. Over the course of a week, he landed his helicopter in insecure and dangerous areas multiple times, neglecting his own safety and saving the lives of countless US soldiers.[8]

Throughout his career, Deane would earn another Distinguished Service Cross, roughly two dozen medals, and the Purple Heart for being wounded in combat. He started as a

Second Lieutenant in 1942, and by the time he retired, he reached the high rank of General.

Deane continued to be promoted several more times until he retired on January 31, 1977. He continued to live for several decades, dying in Bangor, Maine, on July 18, 2013, aged 94.

LEO H. SCHWEITER

Born Leo Henry Schweiter in 1917 in Wichita, Kansas, little is known about his early life. He went to Kansas State College, but not much of his life was recorded until he enlisted in 1941, joining the Army Air Corps before the US joined World War II. Over the course of the war, he initially transferred to the 101st Airborne Division and was promoted to the position of captain. He took part in the Normandy landing on June 6, 1944. He was taken prisoner by the Germans after being injured by a grenade, but was released when the Germans withdrew the next day.[9] He took part in Operation MARKET GARDEN, then the Siege of Bastogne. By the end of the war, he became very confident in the American's ability to defeat the Germans easily, and it was clear that the war was ending. He was in the 7th Infantry Division during the Korean War, taking part in both the Battle of Inchon and Wonsan landings.

He continued to rise through the ranks between the Korean and Vietnam Wars. By November 1967, Schweiter had risen to the rank of Brigadier General, and was in command of the 173rd Airborne Brigade. He reported to General Peers and set up a command post at Ben Het, before impressively leading the brigade into the Battle of Dak To.[10] Schweiter used his tactical know-how to gird the defenses at Dak To I and II and to sweep the Dak Klong Valley south of Ben Het along with an area known as "Rocket Ridge," which the North Vietnamese liked to use as a launching site. Schweiter's command during the Battle of Dak To was characterized by the search for the infamous 66th

Regiment of the PAVN. These were dangerous endeavors, and Schweiter's decades of experience were relied upon as poor decision-making would cost American lives. Schweiter was known as a savvy and cautious tactician who would present General Peers with the qualifying information necessary for the command to make decisions that were in the best interests of the soldiers, as well as the mission at hand. Given the orders by General Peers to take control of the area, Schweiter took control of several hills throughout Dak To. He also used the 173rd to support other units, such as Colonel Johnson's 1st Brigade, whom he aided with evacuations, equipment resupplies, and flanking support while also advancing on territory ordered to be captured by General Peers. On November 23, 1967, Schweiter reaffirmed his commitment to his mission and his men when he had helicopters deliver Thanksgiving dinner to his men after they took control of Hill 875. Despite critiques of this campaign, General Westmorland commanded the efforts of Peers and Schweiter, saying that bottling up the North Vietnamese in the mountainous regions rather than in populated areas was critical to the success of the endeavor.

After being given time to rebuild the unit, he led the Sky Soldiers into Operation BOLLING toward the end of 1967. In 1969, he was given the Distinguished Service Medal for "numerous decisive combat operations against the forces of the VC and North Vietnamese Army," including at "Khe Sanh, the defense of Hue City... and the offensive into the A Shau Valley."[11] Schweiter was lauded for his skills as a tactical commander and a staff director.

Health problems saw him rescind command to Brigadier General Richard Allen early in 1968. He continued as the Chief of Staff, United States Army in Vietnam until May 1972.

When his health worsened, he finally retired in May 1972 and died later that year.[12]

Given how important the Sky Soldiers were during their

years of service in the Vietnam War, the 173rd received a great deal of favorable recognition when they finally returned to the US. Their outstanding performance over the years of brutal fighting and near impossible circumstances was instrumental in many of the strategic campaign successes achieved throughout the war.

8

THE SKY SOLDIERS IN POPULAR CULTURE

The reputation of the Sky Soldiers precedes them in such a way that the unit, not unlike the Green Berets or SEAL Team 6, is mentioned regularly in reverential terms in popular culture, films, and television shows. Some notable examples include Martin Sheen's character Captain Willard from the film *Apocalypse Now* [1], who was a member of the 173rd, Danny Glover's character from the 1987 film *Lethal Weapon*[2], who was also a member of the 173rd, as well as the 2006 song "8th of November" by Big and Rich, which is about Niles Harris' real-life experiences during Operation HUMP.[3]

There is a reason the unit has such a cache in the media. The 173rd is one of the most lauded and celebrated units in military history. Not only that, but they are also colorful, unique, and interesting. They were known as rabble-rousers, fierce fighters, and well-trained combat veterans.

Their reputation followed the Sky Soldiers home, and they gained their due recognition back in the US. The unit has been commemorated over the years for its dedicated professionalism and focus on some of the most difficult combat situations. The

American public continues to honor the spirit and work of the Sky Soldiers to this day.

Few units sacrificed more during the Vietnam War than the 173rd Airborne Brigade. Their proximity to the conflict made them a practical choice as one of the first units to enter the war, but their grit, determination, rigor, and ferocity made them an essential aspect of the planning and execution of multiple operations during the conflict. The 173rd was formed long before Vietnam, and they have existed long after, but the heroism the soldiers in the 173rd displayed during the Vietnam war made them legendary.

CITATIONS AND HONORS

The 173rd Airborne was one of the first Army units deployed to South Vietnam, where they took part in some of the bloodiest conflicts. By the time they were removed from combat, they had earned four unit citations, fourteen campaign streamers, thirteen Medals of Honor, forty-six Distinguished Service Crosses, nearly 2,000 Silver Stars, and more than 6,000 Purple Hearts. They lost 1,647 of their own during the more than six years they were in South Vietnam.

Though the war was not yet over for the US, commanders deactivated the Sky Soldiers in 1972. The US pulled out of the Vietnam war at the end of March 1973. This makes the Sky Soldiers one of the longest-serving Army units of the Vietnam War.

President Lyndon B. Johnson awarded the Sky Soldiers the Presidential Unit Citation on August 4, 1967.[4] According to the released citation, they earned the award for their courage in March 1966 when they conducted search-and-sweep operations, then held a defensive perimeter. The citation is awarded to units that exhibit exceptional heroism while fighting against an enemy. The unit must "display such gallantry, determination, and 'esprit-de-corps' in accomplishing its mission under extremely difficult and hazardous conditions as to set it apart from and above other units in the same campaign."[5]

173RD AIRBORNE BRIGADE MEMORIALS

To commemorate the commendable sacrifices, successes, and legacy of the Sky Soldiers, a fitting memorial was designed and commissioned in the late 1990s by the 173rd Airborne Brigade Association Sigholz Capital Chapter. This group is an organization made up of former members of the 173rd with the purpose of maintaining contact between former members of the 173rd, strengthening the bonds of the current and former members, perpetuating the memory of 173rd Airborne soldiers, and promoting the spirit of the Sky Soldiers. The group felt it was necessary to dedicate a memorial to the 173rd at Arlington National Cemetery.

In May 1998, the memorial was dedicated. The memorial is an inscribed stone devoted specifically to those who served between 1963 and 1971. The memorial includes the following inscription:

> *In commemoration of all Sky Soldiers*
> *Whose valor and sacrifice in defense of*
> *South Vietnam must never be forgotten.*
> *"All Gave Some—Some Gave All*[6]

For nearly ten years, this memorial served as the most well-known and prominent physical memorial to the 173rd. In the early 2000s, however, another memorial was planned. This memorial would expand the scope of who was honored. Over 1,600 sponsors made the memorial possible, including the aforementioned musical act Big & Rich and country rock legends Lynyrd Skynyrd who contributed the proceeds of a "Day of Honor Concert" to help fund the project.[7]

In June 2010, they dedicated the memorial in Columbus, Georgia. The memorial honors not just those who died from 1963 to 1971 but those who have served in Europe, Afghanistan, and beyond. The memorial is also dedicated to the families of the 173rd and the allies who fought alongside the brigade. The memorial's website describes the intention of the memorial as follows:

> "The Memorial is dedicated to all Sky Soldiers who have served or will serve in the 173rd Airborne Brigade. It stands as a tribute to those Sky Soldiers who fell in combat while answering our nation's call. It is equally dedicated, with unwavering gratitude, to those Sky Soldier families who suffered and sacrificed so much in our nation's efforts to preserve freedom. It also recognizes our allies who fell at our side while serving with uncommon valor."[8]

After the dedication of the memorial in Georgia, the memorial that had been at Arlington National Cemetery in Virginia was moved to the Alabama State Veterans Memorial Cemetery in Spanish Fort, Alabama. This original memorial was rededicated and is now along the Memorial Walk with other memorials to Americans who served their country. These memorials are but a small token from a grateful citizenry to a group who sacrificed so much for their country.

CONCLUSION

On June 12, 2000, just in time for the dawn of the 21st century, the 173rd Airborne Brigade was reactivated. The brigade operated in Europe as a part of SETAF—US Army Southern European Task Force—where it conducted various training and exercises.[1]

On March 26, 2003, the 173rd became a part of the Global War on Terrorism when the unit was mobilized as a part of Operation IRAQI FREEDOM.

"As part of what may be the largest airborne assault since D-Day, 20 airmen of the 86th Contingency Response Group parachuted into northern Iraq on March 27 with more than 1,000 soldiers of the 173rd Airborne Brigade.

"The people who jumped into Iraq comprised a team of specialists from the intelligence, medical, communications, security, aerial port, engineer and fuels career fields. Their skills helped prepare the airfield for the C-17 Globemaster IIIs that now deliver more than 1 million pounds of people and cargo every night."[2]

With this parachute jump, as well as many other operations throughout the war in Iraq and beyond, their legacy as the legendary Sky Soldiers continues. The brigade also deployed to Afghanistan as part of Operation ENDURING FREEDOM in 2005. They sent some units of the Sky Soldiers to the border of Pakistan, and the rest went to the Regional Command South. The 173rd lost another seventeen soldiers in 2005. Command deployed more troops to the area in 2007 before in July 2008, the Sky Soldiers were finally removed from the region and sent back to Europe after losing another forty-three soldiers. The unit was redeployed to Afghanistan in 2009 for twelve months and again in 2012, continuing to be active in the Afghanistan war throughout 2013. In 2014, the 173rd found themselves part of Operation ATLANTIC RESOLVE, where they were working with NATO forces to oppose the Russian military actions against Ukraine in 2014.

Even as the unit is reorganized and transformed (now known as an Airborne Infantry Brigade Combat Team or IBCT(A)), it remains one of the most storied and relied upon units in US military history. Said Major General Frank G. Helmick, commander of Southern European Task Force, during a ceremony at Warner Barracks, "The 173rd Airborne Brigade is rich in history, honor, determination, heroism, and end-mission success."[3]

Their contributions to the conflict in Vietnam were not the unit's first forays into heroism, and it will not be their last, though their contributions to that war should never be forgotten. By the time they were removed from Vietnam, they had lost over 1,600 of their own, and many others suffered life-changing injuries. The sacrifices they made have earned them the respect of the country they served with honor.

Beyond the missions and their contribution to American military operations, the Sky Soldiers are representative of the bond soldiers form when they serve together. Thousands of soldiers from across the US have served in the 173rd and made sacrifices of all kinds for their country, their military, and one another.

One way this is honored is with the event called "The Running of the Herd." This event is an annual race and memorial to honor fallen Sky Soldiers from Vietnam and other engagements. It is run on November 8th to remember the sacrifices made on November 8, 1965, during Operation HUMP.[4] The event is a team relay race, and the name refers to the Sky Soldier's original nickname, "the herd," that they earned by playing Rawhide at reveille.

When asked about the tradition, Tim Austin, a former member of the 173rd Airborne Brigade, explained, "It's like a brotherhood (most people) can never understand."[4]

To any Sky Soldier who picked up this book....
Thank you for your service

To the reader: If you have a spare moment, I would sincerely welcome your book review and any comments you may have. With thanks.

VIETNAM TIMELINE

The following provides a timeline of French occupation through the departure of the Sky Soldiers from the Vietnam War.

1858	France begins attacking Vietnam.
1862	France takes control of Vietnam.
May 1929	The Indochinese Communist Party forms in Hong Kong.
February 1930	Ho Chi Minh returns to Vietnam to oversee the formation of the party in Vietnam.
September 26, 1940	Japan invades and takes control of Vietnam from the French.
May 1941	Ho Chi Minh helps found the League for the Independence of Vietnam.
1941 to 1945	The US sends agents to assist Ho Chi Minh to fight the Japanese in Vietnam.
1945	Japan executes most French officials.

August 6, 1945   An atomic bomb destroys Hiroshima.

August 9, 1945   An atomic bomb destroys Nagasaki.

August 1945   Japan surrenders, ending World War II. They leave Vietnam.

1945 to 1954   Ho Chi Minh and his troops continue to fight South Vietnamese to gain Vietnam's Independence.

July 1954   France leaves Vietnam.

August 2, 1964   The Gulf of Tonkin incident occurs.

August 7, 1964   US Congress passes the *Gulf of Tonkin Resolution*, authorizing the use of force in Vietnam.

1965   The Sky Soldiers are among the first soldiers deployed to Vietnam.

May 5, 1965   The Sky Soldiers begin arriving in Vietnam and are sent to War Zone D.

November 5 to 8, 1965   Operation HUMP conducted.

January 1 to 8, 1966   Operation MARAUDER conducted.

January 8 to 14, 1966   Operation CRIMP conducted.

May 10 to August 1, 1966   Operation PAUL REVERE conducted.

February 12 to April 5, 1967   Operation SAM HOUSTON conducted.

February 22 to May 14, 1967   Operation JUNCTION CITY conducted.

April 6 to October 11, 1967   Operation FRANCIS MARION conducted.

June 17 to October 11, 1967   Operation GREELEY conducted.

November 1967   The Battle of Hill 875 takes place.

October 12, 1967   Operation MACARTHUR begins.

January 30 and 31, 1968   The Tet Offensive begins.

February 24, 1968   The first phase of the Tet Offensive ends.

January 31, 1969   Operation MACARTHUR ends.

1972   The Sky Soldiers are deactivated.

2000   The Sky Soldiers are reactivated for the European theater and then the War on Terror in the Middle East

REFERENCES

INTRODUCTION

1. AnySoldier.com. "173d Airborne Brigade 'Sky Soldiers,'" n.d. http://anysoldier.com/brian/About173.html.

2. Danker, Brian and Corey, Steve. "Wild Times With N Company, 75th Infantry Regiment: Serving With The 173rd In Vietnam," by David Siry. The West Point Center for Oral History. March 31, 2022. https://www.westpointcoh.org/interviews/wild-times-with-n-company-75th-infantry-regiment-serving-with-the-173rd-in-vietnam.

3. McNeir, D. Kevin. "Former Airborne Brigade Soldier Lawrence Boyd Sr. Visits Vietnam Veterans Memorial." The Washington Informer, April 27, 2022. https://www.washingtoninformer.com/former-airborne-brigade-soldier-lawrence-boyd-sr-visits-vietnam-veterans-memorial/.

4. Danker, Brian and Corey, Steve. "Wild Times With N Company, 75th Infantry Regiment: Serving With The

173rd In Vietnam," by David Siry. The West Point Center for Oral History. March 31, 2022. https://www.westpointcoh.org/interviews/wild-times-with-n-company-75th-infantry-regiment-serving-with-the-173rd-in-vietnam.

CHAPTER 1

1. Rotondi, Jessica. "6 Events That Laid the Groundwork for the Vietnam War." History.com, August 20, 2020. https://www.history.com/news/vietnam-war-origins-events

2. Lindsay, James. "The Vietnam War in 40 Quotes." *The National Interest*, April 30, 2015. https://nationalinterest.org/blog/the-buzz/the-vietnam-war-40-quotes-12776.

3. . Woolf, Chris. "The Little-Known Story of Vietnamese Communist Leader Ho Chi Minh's." The World From PRX, September 18, 2017. https://theworld.org/stories/2017-09-18/little-known-story-vietnamese-communist-leader-ho-chi-minh-s-admiration-us

4. History.com Editors. "THIS DAY IN HISTORY OCTOBER 11, 1954 October 11 Viet Minh Take Control in the North." History.com, November 16, 2009. https://www.history.com/this-day-in-history/viet-minh-take-control-in-the-north

5. Thế Anh, Nguyễn. "Bao Dai's Abdication and the Failure of an Imperial Project." End of Empire, February 12, 2016. https://www.endofempire.asia/0830-bao-dais-abdication-and-the-failure-of-the-imperial-project-2/

6. 4b. Sheldon, George F. "Status of the Viet Nam." Far Eastern Survey, December 18, 1946. https://doi.org/10.2307/3021292

7. Wise, Edward Tayloe. Vietnam in Turmoil: The Japanese Coup, the OSS, and the August Revolution in 1945. University of Richmond UR Scholarship Repository, 1991. https://scholarship.richmond.edu/cgi/viewcontent.cgi?article=2335&context=masters-theses

8. Bartholomew-Feis, Dixee. "The OSS in Vietnam, 1945: A War of Missed Opportunities by Dixee Bartholomew-Feis." The National WWII Museum | New Orleans, July 14, 2020. https://www.nationalww2museum.org/war/articles/oss-vietnam-1945-dixee-bartholomew-feis

9. Alpha History. "Mao Zedong," June 14, 2019. https://alphahistory.com/vietnamwar/mao-zedong/

10. Leeson, Peter T., and Andrea M. Dean. "The Democratic Domino Theory: An Empirical Investigation." *American Journal of Political Science* 53, no. 3 (July 2009): 533–51. https://doi.org/10.1111/j.1540-5907.2009.00385.x

11. History.com Editors. "THIS DAY IN HISTORY MAY 07, 1954 May 07 French Defeated at Dien Bien Phu." History.com, February 9, 2010. https://www.history.com/this-day-in-history/french-defeated-at-dien-bien-phu

12. Greenspan, Jesse. "How the Vietnam War Ratcheted Up Under 5 US Presidents Truman, Eisenhower, Kennedy, Johnson and Nixon All Deepened US Involvement in the Decades-Long Conflict." History.com, March 14, 2019. https://www.history.com/news/us-presidents-vietnam-war-escalation.

CHAPTER 2

1. Lindsay, James. "TWE Remembers: The First US Combat Troops Arrive in Vietnam." Council on Foreign Relations, March 8, 2015. https://www.cfr.org/blog/twe-remembers-first-us-combat-troops-arrive-vietnam

2. HISTORY.COM EDITORS. "Operation ROLLING THUNDER." History.com, February 24, 2010. Accessed February 23, 2023. https://www.history.com/topics/vietnam-war/operation-rolling-thunder

3. Glass, Andrew. "LBJ Approves 'Operation ROLLING THUNDER,' Feb. 13, 1965." POLITICO, February 13, 2019. https://www.politico.com/story/2019/02/13/lbj-operation-rolling-thunder-feb-13-1965-1162618.

4. 173rd Airborne Brigade. "173rd Airborne Brigade: About Us: Our History." 173rd Airborne Brigade, n.d. https://www.skysoldiers.army.mil/About-Us/Our-History/

5. Howard, John. "Going to War in 1965 with the Army You Have." HistoryNet, December 20, 2019. https://www.historynet.com/going-to-war-in-1965-with-the-army-you-have/.

6. 173rd Airborne Brigade. "173rd Airborne Brigade: About Us: Our History." 173rd Airborne Brigade, n.d. https://www.skysoldiers.army.mil/About-Us/Our-History/

7. https://www.globalsecurity.org/military/agency/army/173abnbde.htm

8. History.com Editors. "THIS DAY IN HISTORY MAY 03 1965 May 03 173rd Airborne Brigade Deploys to South Vietnam." History.com, November 16, 2009. https://www.history.com/this-day-in-history/173rd-airborne-brigade-deploys-to-south-vietnam.

9. Click Americana. "Vietnam War Map: Corps to Corps (1968)," October 10, 2019. https://clickamericana. com/topics/war-topics/vietnam-war-map-corps-to-corps-1968

CHAPTER 3

1. donors@asomf.org. "Operation HUMP." ASOMF, November 29, 2022. https://www.asomf.org/ operation-hump/
2. Wilkins, Warren. "How Did Vietnamese Forces Block US Firepower? With a Hug." HistoryNet, February 17, 2023. https://www.historynet.com/vietnam-hugging-tactics/.
3. Tolson, John. Vietnam Studies - Airmobility 1961-1971. Zaltbommel, Netherlands: Van Haren Publishing, 1999.
4. Staff, HistoryNet. "Operation Marauder: Allied Offensive in the Mekong Delta." HistoryNet, August 8, 2016. https://www.historynet.com/operation-marauder-allied-offensive-in-the-mekong-delta.htm
5. 50th Anniversary of the Vietnam War. "Week of December 30 - January 5th," 2015. https://www. vietnamwar50th.com/education/week_of_january_7/.

CHAPTER 4

1. Hand, George. "Operation Junction City: Vietnam's Only Large-Scale Airborne Operation." Sandboxx, May 27, 2022. https://www.sandboxx.us/blog/ operation-junction-city-vietnams-only-large-scale-airborne-operation/

2. History.com. "Cu Chi Tunnels," August 2011. https://www.history.com/topics/vietnam-war/cu-chi-tunnels

3. 16th Infantry Regiment Association. "Operation CEDAR FALLS 9-16 January 1967 | 16th Infantry Regiment Association," n.d. https://16thinfassn.org/history/regimental-maps/vietnam-cold-war-ii-1965-1990/operation-cedar-falls-9-16-january-1967/

4. History, Alpha. "Cambodia." Vietnam War, January 8, 2023. https://alphahistory.com/vietnamwar/cambodia/

5. Hand, George. "Operation Junction City: Vietnam's Only Large-Scale Airborne Operation." Sandboxx, May 27, 2022. https://www.sandboxx.us/blog/operation-junction-city-vietnams-only-large-scale-airborne-operation/

6. Grundhauser, Eric. "The Myth of the Bamboo Pentagon: The Vietnam War's Phantom Enemy Headquarters." Atlas Obscura, June 10, 2021. https://www.atlasobscura.com/articles/the-myth-of-the-bamboo-pentagon-the-fabled-viet-cong-headquarters-that-pushed-america-into-cambodia.

7. 16th Infantry Regiment Association. "Operation JUNCTION CITY 22 February-15 April 1967 | 16th Infantry Regiment Association," n.d. https://16thinfassn.org/history/regimental-maps/vietnam-cold-war-ii-1965-1990/operation-junction-city-22-february-15-april-1967/

8. https://apps.dtic.mil/dtic/tr/fulltext/u2/a139612.pdf

9. Dinh Thi Van. *I Engaged in Intelligence Work (The Many Faces of Viet Nam)*. The Gioi Publishers, 2006.

10. Paschall, Rod. "Dark Clouds Over Junction City." HistoryNet, February 9, 2016. https://www.historynet.com/dark-clouds-over-junction-city/

11. Hand, George. "Operation Junction City: Vietnam's Only Large-Scale Airborne Operation." Sandboxx, May 27, 2022. https://www.sandboxx.us/blog/operation-junction-city-vietnams-only-large-scale-airborne-operation/

12. US Military & Insignia Manufacturer: The Salute Uniforms. "US ARMY 173RD AIRBORNE BRIGADE COMBAT TEAM UNIT CREST (DUI)," n.d. http://www.uniforms-4u.com/p-army-173-airborne-brigade-unit-crest-8781.aspx.

CHAPTER 5

1. History.com. "Vietnam War Protests," February 10, 2010. https://www.history.com/topics/vietnam-war/vietnam-war-protests

2. Brown, Jim. "Why Did President Johnson Entered the Vietnam War? – KnowledgeBurrow.Com," April 21, 2021. https://knowledgeburrow.com/why-did-president-johnson-entered-the-vietnam-war/

3. Clarke, Jeffrey. *Advice and Support: The Final Years, 1965-1973 (United States Army in Vietnam Cmh Pub Ser, Cmh Pub No, 91-3)*. Center of Military History, 1998. pp. 37-38. https://history.army.mil/banner_images/focus/dr_clarke_ret_comm/the_final_years.pdf

4. "The VVA Veteran, a Publication of Vietnam Veterans of America," n.d. https://vvaveteran.org/32-1/32-1_dakto67.html

5. Sheehan, Neil. "Opinion | David and Goliath in Vietnam." The New York Times, June 4, 2017. https://www.nytimes.com/2017/05/26/opinion/sunday/david-and-goliath-in-vietnam.html

6. MacGarrigle, George and Center of Military History. Combat Operations: Taking the Offensive, October

1966 to October 1967. Center of Military History, US Army, 1998. https://history.army.mil/html/books/ 091/91-4/index.html

7. Lindsay, James. "TWE Remembers: General Westmoreland Says the 'End Begins to Come Into View' in Vietnam." Council on Foreign Relations, November 21, 2017. https://www.cfr.org/blog/twe-remembers-general-westmoreland-says-end-begins-come-view-vietnam

8. The Virtual Wall: Vietnam Veterans Memorial. "Hill 830: July 1967," July 1, 2013. https://www.virtualwall.org/units/hill830.htm

CHAPTER 6

1. The Hall of Valor Project. "Carlos Lozada - Recipient -," n.d. https://valor.militarytimes.com/hero/310

2. Ismay, John. "The Secret History of a Vietnam War Airstrike Gone Terribly Wrong." *The New York Times*, February 4, 2019. https://www.nytimes.com/2019/ 01/31/magazine/vietnam-war-airstrike-dak-to.html

3. Cranford Historic Preservation Advisory Board. "Chaplain Major Charles Watters," 2014. http:// preservecranford.com/index.html

4. Ismay, John. "The Secret History of a Vietnam War Airstrike Gone Terribly Wrong." *The New York Times*, February 4, 2019. https://www.nytimes.com/2019/ 01/31/magazine/vietnam-war-airstrike-dak-to.html

5. Hall of Valor Project. "Dwight Johnson - Recipient -," n.d. https://valor.militarytimes.com/hero/683

6. McCrumb, Vance. "Vietnam War Statistics." *Vietnam Veterans of America,* n.d. https://www.vva310.org/ vietnam-war-statistics

7. John Andrew Barnes, III (April 16, 1945 — November 12, 1967) | World Biographical Encyclopedia (prabook.com)

CHAPTER 7

1. Ratcliffe, Susan. Oxford Essential Quotations. Oxford University Press, 2017. https://www.oxfordreference.com/display/10.1093/acref/9780191843730.001.0001/q-oro-ed5-00011305;jsessionid=58AFCAF6B7673D50FBF80CA63C0C91BD

2. Hickman, Kennedy. "Vietnam War and the Battle of Dak To." ThoughtCo, October 3, 2019. https://www.thoughtco.com/vietnam-war-nixon-and-vietnamization-p2-2361339

3. Together We Served. "Shadow Box: Peers, William Ray, LTG," n.d. https://army.togetherweserved.com/army/servlet/tws.webapp.WebApp?cmd=ShadowBoxProfile&type=BattleMemoryExt&ID=116215

4. Erik, Villard. *Staying the Course - October 1967 to September 1968: United States Army in Vietnam Combat Operations, Official Comprehensive History of Battles in Southeast Asia Against VC and North Vietnamese.* Center of Military History United States Army, 2018. https://history.army.mil/html/books/091/91-15-1/index.html

5. "Biography of General William R. Peers," https://web.archive.org/web/19990427192242/http://www.law.umkc.edu/faculty/projects/ftrials/mylai/myl_bpeers.htm

6. Thompson, Hugh. "Moral Courage In Combat: The My Lai Story (Speech)." USNA.edu, 2003. Accessed March 7, 2022. William C. Stutt Ethics Lecture. Annapolis, MD. Archived from the original (PDF) on

February 21, 2007. Retrieved March 7, 2022. https://web.archive.org/web/20070221172507/https://www.usna.edu/Ethics/publications/ThompsonPg1-28_Final.pdf

7. Deane, John R. "Growing Up as an Army Brat." In *Lessons in Leadership: My Life in the US Army from World War II to Vietnam*, edited by Jack C. Mason, 1–15. University Press of Kentucky, 2018. https://doi.org/10.2307/j.ctt22p7j74.4

8. The Hall of Valor Project. "John Deane - Recipient -," n.d. https://valor.militarytimes.com/hero/7490

9. Koskimaki, George. *D-Day with the Screaming Eagles.* Casemate, 2008.

10. Erik, Villard. *Staying the Course - October 1967 to September 1968: United States Army in Vietnam Combat Operations, Official Comprehensive History of Battles in Southeast Asia Against VC and North Vietnamese.* Center of Military History United States Army, 2018.

11. The Hall of Valor Project. "Leo Schweiter - Recipient -," n.d. https://valor.militarytimes.com/hero/111933

12. Murphy, Edward. Dak To: America's Sky Soldiers in South Vietnam's Central Highlands. Presidio Press, 2008.

CHAPTER 8

1. *Apocalypse Now*. Hollywood, California: Paramount Pictures. 1979.

2. *Lethal Weapon*. Warner Bros. 1987.

3. Crevier, Scott. "8th of November–A Small Gesture to Show Gratitude and Respect for America's Vietnam Vets.," n.d. https://www.8thofnovember.com/

4. Peters, Gerhard, and John Woolley. "Presidential Unit Citation Awarded the 2d Battalion (Airborne), 503d

Infantry, 173d Airborne Brigade (Separate), USA, and Attached Units | The American Presidency Project." The American Presidency Project, n.d. https://www. presidency.ucsb.edu/documents/presidential-unit-citation-awarded-the-2d-battalion-airborne-503d-infantry-173d-airborne

5. TracesOfWar.com. "Distinguished Unit Citation / Presidential Unit Citation," n.d. https://www. tracesofwar.com/awards/540/Distinguished-Unit-Citation---Presidential-Unit-Citation.htm?sort= changed

6. Hilton, Mark. "173d Airborne Brigade (Sep)." Historical Marker Database, January 18, 2017. https://www.hmdb.org/m.asp?m=100946

7. 173d Airborne Brigade National Memorial Foundation. "173rd Airborne Brigade Memorial Foundation Funding," June 21, 2020. https://www. 173dairbornememorial.org/funding/

8. 173d Airborne Brigade National Memorial Foundation. "173rd Airborne Brigade National Memorial | National Infantry Museum in Columbus GA," July 7, 2017. https://www. 173dairbornememorial.org/the-memorial/

CONCLUSION

1. GlobalSecurity.org. "173rd Airborne Brigade," 2008. http://www.globalsecurity.org/military/agency/army/ 173abnbde.htm

2. Ulmer, Phillip. "Airmen Jump in, Prepare Airfield in Northern Iraq." Air Force, April 2, 2003. https:// www.af.mil/News/Article-Display/Article/139613/ airmen-jump-in-prepare-airfield-in-northern-iraq/

3. Aird, Brandon. "173rd Airborne Brigade Becomes a Brigade Combat Team." www.army.mil, September 18, 2006. https://www.army.mil/article/166

4. Montgomery, Nancy. "'Running of the Herd' Honors GIs Who Fought in Vietnam Battle." Stars and Stripes, November 7, 2013. https://www.stripes.com/news/running-of-the-herd-honors-gis-who-fought-in-vietnam-battle-1.251649

ABOUT THE AUTHOR

Charles J. McArthur is a retired journalist who was born and raised in West Virginia, before venturing out on a life of travels. He spent much of his later career working and living in Asia, where he raised his own family. Having had a lifelong interest in military history, he now spends his retirement researching and writing on the subject, so the true stories of courage and bravery may never be forgotten.